shift WITH INTENTION

...AND SOAR!

YOUR GUIDE TO MANIFESTING YOUR BEST LIFE

COMPILED BY

JAIME ZOGRAFOS

Shift with Intention...and Soar!
Your Guide to Manifesting Your Best Life
Jaime Zografos
Two Wizards Publishing

Published by Two Wizards Publishing, St. Louis, MO
Copyright ©2022 Jaime Zografos
All rights reserved.

Editor/Writing Coach: Cheryl Roberts

Proofreader: Angela Houston, ahouston@ahjoyediting.com

Cover and Interior design: Davis Creative Publishing Partners, CreativePublishingPartners.com

Library of Congress Cataloging-in-Publication Data

Library of Congress Control Number: 2022906760

Jaime Zografos
Shift with Intention...and Soar!: Your Guide to Manifesting Your Best Life

ISBN: 979-8-9859287-0-9 (paperback)
        979-8-9859287-1-6 (hardback)
        979-8-9859287-2-3 (ebook)

2022

ATTENTION CORPORATIONS, UNIVERSITIES, COLLEGES AND PROFESSIONAL ORGANIZATIONS: Quantity discounts are available on bulk purchases of this book for educational, gift purposes, or as premiums for increasing magazine subscriptions or renewals. Special books or book excerpts can also be created to fit specific needs. For information, please contact Two Wizards Publishing, info@TwoWizardsPublishing.Com.

DEDICATION

This book is dedicated to Rich Dreyer. Rich was a clever, comical, thoughtful, and incredibly caring man to so many. For me, Rich was like a father, as well as a mentor and dear friend. He knew nearly everything about me and never passed judgment. He added the word "Soar" and the seagull to the cover of this book while we were designing it, giving it very special meaning. Rich always had his hands in something. Rich was always helping others get through their struggles and calling them out if they needed to see something they could not see. He taught me how to love and value myself.

Dreyer, I hope you are flying high and smiling down
on those lives you continue to touch!

Wiz, I love you and I am forever grateful
for our beautiful time together.
Love, Junior Wiz

ACKNOWLEDGMENTS

My intention with this anthology was to attract the right people to share their story to help provide hope and a collection of ideas for others to start to learn how to shift their lives. I am humbled by the authors who have chosen to be in this collection of stories. Each is handpicked to bring different insights. I am grateful for each and every one of them. This book would not be possible had they not believed in me and my mission for the book. Each one of these authors has a giving heart. This incredible project has been sourced from a higher power, and I am simply the facilitator; in that, I am humbled and grateful for this opportunity.

Love,

Jaime Zografos

CHERYL ROBERTS

Just as Well

A child pretends, blends, observes,
learns everyone is angry or afraid.
Wishing to be unseen, she decides

to hide her real self. It's easy.
Battered by momentum,
no one really sees, so she decides

motion will be added to her disguise,
reasoning, if she's always on her way,
no one will know if she never arrives.

Then one day, she wondered if her real self,
the one that she'd been keeping safe,
had been misplaced?

So long ignored, denied, deprived,
she decides it's time to excavate
her sacred bits and pieces.

She shivered as she realized, who she
might have been will never be,
then decides, "Just as well, it's for the best."

Now she can be the woman she's become,
this imperfect one she finally learned
to trust and love.

TABLE OF CONTENTS

Your Unwritten Chapter

Why do we do things the hard way?
Why do we try to go through closed doors?
Why do we struggle to get things we don't even truly want?
Why do we make choices that are not good for us?
Why do we miss opportunities?

Because we are stuck. We do this, until one day, we SHIFT.

Are YOU ready to make your shift?

Are you ready to start finding an easier way to do things? To find the new door that is open and actually walk through it? To stop struggling for what you don't want or need? To make healthier choices for ourselves? To take advantage of opportunities that you once missed?

Where is that SHIFT?

This book is for the version of you that is ready to answer: "Where is my shift?"

Your next chapter is unwritten. You are ready to write the next chapter of your life with the intention to shift something! You are the only one that can write it! Start by figuring out, where is it you want to SHIFT?

My Shift

It's June 2009. Sydney is nine years old, and Sophie is five. We are leaving Sydney's softball game at 9:00 p.m.

Sydney says, "Mom, can I sit in the front seat on the way home tonight?"

"No, Sydney, we are going to be on a long and winding road, and it is much safer in the back seat, babe. Put your seat belt on while I get Sophie buckled up."

I did not listen to my own advice about getting my seat belt on.

A minute later, we are headed down a ravine off Pond Road and I am being thrown all over the front seat of the 2007 Chevy Suburban. The car slams into a tree. I turn around and ask the girls if they are OK.

They say, "Yes! Mom, we are fine, but your face?"

I said, "I need to find my phone! We need to get help!"

Something draws our attention. We all look outside the driver-side window and see a man standing there. He had a brown beard and was wearing white robes.

He calmly says, "Help is on the way!"

I said, "Do you have a phone?"

He repeated, "Help is on the way!" and then was gone. We never saw him again.

Within minutes, two ambulances were there to take us to the hospital, the girls in one and me in the other. The girls were unharmed. I was not. My left wrist was shattered, my left foot broken, and my face had smashed into the steering wheel, ruining my front teeth.

It was the middle of the night. The girls walked out without a scratch. I was pushed out in a wheelchair, feeling overwhelmingly grateful for my intuition telling me Sydney should be in the back seat. Days later, my wrist was put back together with a plate and seven screws, my foot in a cast, and my face still missing the bright-toothed smile of which I'd been so proud.

Back in 2009, I did not have the level of awareness that I do now. Now I know:

Car accidents are the Universe's way of letting you know
you are going the wrong direction.

I was in three car accidents between June and September 2009. The Universe gets loud with me when I don't listen! I continued along that path, trying to go through closed doors.

The next sign was six years later, in 2015. I had breast cancer. This was loud enough for me to hear it. **It was my first SHIFT!**

From 2016 to 2020, I learned how to dive into my questions and find answers. People, places, and things showed up to lead me! I got to choose whether to go through the open door or bang against the familiar closed door.

I set an intention to learn how the mind works! Why did I get cancer? Why I was in a terrible accident? Why did I fail at two marriages before I was forty years old?

Intention is a powerful term used to determine how things are going to play out for you, your goal, or your aim.

How do we set our intention and achieve our goals? Here's what I did:

- I wrote three affirmations every single night ten times each, for a year.
- I took every personal development workshop I could get my hands on.
- I hired coaches.
- I went to therapists.
- I journaled.
- I looked in the mirror every day and told myself "I love you!"
- I talked with my mentor regularly about everything.
- I listened to eight hours of reprogramming the subconscious mind on you tube while I slept for three months straight.
- I said daily mantras to change my mindset.
- I read every book recommended to me on personal development.
- I paid over $100,000 to travel with Tony Robbins, attending every course he offered in 2018.
- I went to a meditation retreat with Joe Dispenza in 2020.

I was doing better. Every year I did a little better. I was attracting things and people into my life that were of value. I was starting to make better choices. But I was not there, not yet.

Shift— a slight change in position, direction, or tendency

I live on three acres with many trees; therefore, I have a lot of leaves!

I was leaf blowing this past fall, one of my most favorite pastimes. Leaf blowing puts me in a different state of mind. What is so wonderful about leaf blowing is when all the leaves move quickly in the same direction that you are blowing. It is so satisfying!

What is not wonderful about leaf blowing is when they all go in opposite directions, fly into my face, over my head, going everywhere but where I want them to go. When this started happening last fall, I chose to turn around and blow the leaves in the direction the wind was blowing. It was so simple, the leaves quickly glided across the yard and into their new home for the winter.

I thought to myself, "This is life!" This is what happens when I go through the door that has been opened, not the closed door that I've been trying to pry open for the seventh time. This message was satisfyingly clear:

Life gets easier when we follow the way the Universe guides us.

Finally, in October 2021, I stopped living in fear of the shame that I was holding and hiding. I stopped looking at my life the "way it was supposed to look." I stopped pressing "play" on the recorded story I ran through my head every single day. It was all because I wrote a chapter in another book, much like this, that unbeknownst to me was healing and freeing.

What I learned writing that chapter was that I had been holding onto feelings that had kept me stuck my whole life: **pain, fear, shame, judgement, and embarrassment.** I was stuck because of what happened to me as a child, something that I had no control over. I realized those feelings had kept me doing the same thing over and over. I thought about Brené Brown's take on shame and vulnerability. Brené says that shame dissipates once we are vulnerable about what makes us feel the shame.

After I released the story, I was a little scared to have people read it. I did not want people to look at me differently, and I did not want people to feel sorry for me. I felt a deep desire to get that chapter out of my head and onto paper. In doing so, I had made myself vulnerable. But I had no idea it would **SHIFT** my entire world.

It Set Me Free

The doors that have opened, people who have walked into my life, opportunities that have been presented to me, the peaceful life I have created and the dreams I am pursuing—none of them, and I mean *none* of them, would be here without the intention to shift and soar!

When I was in the accident, going through two divorces and surviving breast cancer, I had no idea where to turn. That is what motivated me to create a resource guide on how people can shift with intention and soar, which leads to manifesting their best life. I want others to have hope, to have help, to have somewhere to turn and a possible path to go on.

I've learned that when life puts up roadblocks, consider looking at them differently. We do not need to push through every roadblock and fight every single battle. Life is here to teach us, and then we get to help others with what we've learned.

When the same lesson keeps reappearing in your life, it is the Universe's way of letting you know you have not learned the lesson, that it is time to start listening.

What is your unwritten chapter?

If life is going in too many or the wrong directions—like the leaves—turn around with your proverbial leaf blower and start going that direction. Start your next chapter! SHIFT and open the damn door!

Jaime Zografos is an entrepreneur engaged in real estate valuation, health and wellness centers, a subscription box business, and retreats. A two-time international best-selling author, Jaime's entrepreneurial career began in the nineties when she founded her real estate appraisal company in the Greater St. Louis region. Her reputation and strong work ethic led to exponential business growth across multiple endeavors. She opened the first of two OsteoStrong franchises in 2018, providing innovative solutions to assist clients in improvement of muscle and bone density, and ultimately enhancing their quality of life. Jaime founded Bountiful Bundles in 2021—a luxury subscription box model curating personalized experiences around manifestation, abundance, and gratitude. Her Bountiful Academy and Retreat Community reflects Jaime's vision of inspiring people to radically transform their lives through fun, challenging, and energizing ways. This particular business was largely inspired by Jaime's story of shifting with intentionality. She hopes to touch the lives of many by inspiring deep personal shifts in others.

www.jaimezenterprises.com/
hello@abundancedelivered.com
www.linkedin.com/in/jaime-zografos-8693a9a6/
www.facebook.com/jaime.ladendorf/

It's Brave to Change Your Mind

Nothing will ruin your twenties more than thinking you should already have your life together.

Graduating high school as an overachieving valedictorian, I went to college with a plan. I was going to be a therapist, and I knew exactly how to make it happen. I mapped out my classes, had research experience lined up, and started volunteering as an on-call victim advocate several nights a month. I presented research at national conferences and maintained perfect grades. I was focused and determined.

On a whim at the end of my sophomore year of college, I signed up to study abroad in Italy and Greece. It was the most exhilarating, transformative experience of my life. Bonus: now I could add a travel section to my resume.

When I got back from Europe, I traded my retail job for one in social services, working eighty-hour weekly shifts in a group home for teenage girls. I was only two years older than some of the girls, but that hardly mattered. I had goals. Taking care of them full time while going to school myself led to sixteen-hour days and added "two years of full-time work in my field" to my growing resume. Sure, it was a lot, but I was the girl who did a lot. And did it perfectly.

I said "yes" to everything: extra shifts, extra projects, extra classes. My health was a small price to pay for being the best. At nineteen, I hadn't found a way to deal with my experiences as an advocate and caretaker where I saw the effects of violence, neglect, and drug use. I dealt with suicide attempts and self-harm. I helped with restraining orders and emergency escape plans. I didn't know how to take care of myself or set boundaries, only focusing on my end goal. The stress left me with ulcers, insomnia, and a drinking problem. Blacking out at the bar after work had become my preferred method for dealing with the mounting stress.

But none of that mattered. I was going to graduate with honors, a perfect GPA, two bachelor's degrees, years of research and field experience, publications in psychology, and over six hundred volunteer hours. I got a rush being able to juggle everything. Every time someone said, "I don't know how you do it all," I secretly felt proud, like I must be doing something right. But it was an unsustainable pace.

As one might anticipate, it took one unexpected bump in the road to lead me to a complete breakdown. Looking back, I'm mostly surprised it took until my senior year for it to happen.

Instead of studying for my exam to get into graduate school to pursue my PhD, I was skipping class to be at work with my girls in the group home, the boundaries between work and my home life now nonexistent. When I took the exam, I tanked an entire section. Getting below-average test results broke me. I had never failed at anything school-related. It was too late to retake the test, having pushed it to the final deadline. All that effort to have the perfect resume, and now I would not be going to graduate school. While it seemed like I was a smart, capable young woman, I now had evidence of my biggest fear—I was a complete failure.

Did I stop to process that and take some things off my plate? Of course not. I needed to start achieving again. Deciding I didn't really want to pursue psychology, I switched to law school. Did I actually want to be a lawyer? I didn't know. I hadn't given it more than five minutes thought before deciding this profession was going to restore my identity as the successful girl who could do it all.

I graduated and got a job at a law firm where I planned to work for one year while applying to law school. It was a respectable plan. I'd make connections, learn from the partners, and get back on track in no time. I was turning my life around. What I didn't plan on was hating every minute of working at a law firm. It was somehow stressful and boring at the same time. At least when I had decided to be a therapist, I had put thought into doing something I loved. I missed helping people and having meaningful interactions. I spent the next nine months so discouraged and depressed that many nights I came home from work and went straight to bed.

I was spiraling, and my now-husband was worried. (Yes, I had also decided to throw a wedding into the chaos of my life.) After watching me struggle for months, he asked me about the last time I was happy. I thought back to the only thing I had done *just for me* and not to boost my resume—studying abroad in Europe.

I had explored castles in Tuscany, watched artists in Venice, went sailing in Santorini, prayed at the Vatican, and made a friend who would later be in my wedding. There was nothing about that trip that really contributed to my career goals, and yet it was the best thing I had ever done.

After that experience, I traveled when I could between school and work, but not as much as I wanted. Ironically, when life gets chaotic, it's the things that make us feel alive that are the first to go. I'd always wanted to travel. As a kid, I would tear up my father's *National Geographic* magazines, hanging maps and gorgeous landscapes on my bedroom walls. Before I had decided I needed to be a complete success by the age of twenty-two, my passion had been about seeing the world. I wanted to visit ancient cities, hike mountains, and learn how to surf.

Remembering all of this, I realized that if all my planning hadn't exactly worked out, I could at least aim for being happy. So I decided to shift from what I thought my life would look like to a life I was excited about.

I emailed the owner of the travel agency that had planned my honeymoon and begged for a job. I had no experience, no idea what the job entailed, and I didn't even live in the same state, but she took a chance on me. Maybe my desperation came off as enthusiasm. Either way, I became a travel agent. It was the first time I was excited about something since my dream of graduate school fell through.

It was hard to get started in a field that I knew nothing about, but I absolutely loved it. I was back to helping people, even if it looked a little different. I had opportunities for my own travels and the flexibility of working from anywhere. I was happy.

Less than six months after taking that job, my husband went to the doctor for a routine checkup. They found a lump in his throat. Not long after the biopsy, we got the call. He had thyroid cancer, and it had spread. A week later, I got a call that my yearly checkup showed I was developing cervical cancer at a rapid pace and would need surgery to stop the growth. My husband had his surgery the day before his twenty-eighth birthday, then radiation on our first wedding anniversary. I had surgery three weeks later. I was twenty-three.

All of this confirmed my new insight: life is way too short to be miserable. With all the stories of people on their deathbeds talking about what matters in the end—family, friends, and experiences—why do most of us carry on with our day-to-day, putting work and achievements first, telling ourselves that it won't be like this forever?

Fortunately, my husband and I had full recoveries. Three years later, I'm still helping others see the world, creating memories that will stay with them forever. I take every opportunity to travel and try something new. I'm still the girl that says "yes" to everything, it just looks different now. I know my adventures and the people I meet along the way are what will matter in the end, not degrees or prestigious careers.

The problem wasn't that I struggled with my identity in college. It was that I thought that by age twenty-two I needed to have everything figured out and was a failure if I didn't. I could have kept going with my plan for psychology or law school, soldiering through, telling myself I'd already committed, already put in the time, already told people my plans...or I could shift.

I chose to live a *life that makes me happy, whatever it looks like and wherever it takes me.* I've learned it's brave to change your mind. It's brave to grow into the person you were meant to be, living fully and authentically, no matter how unconventional it looks. What matters is making sure we are actually *living* our lives, not just creating outward appearances.

Cally Conyers grew up in Belle, Missouri with parents who cultivated her love of learning at a young age. She is the eldest of three with two exceptional younger siblings. She attended college at Missouri State University, graduating with a double major in psychology and philosophy. Since becoming a travel agent, she has traveled to multiple countries, learned how to surf, hiked several mountain ranges, and even traveled around the world solo a couple of times. Younger Cally would be proud. In addition to being a travel agent, she discovered a passion for helping people in fitness and now works part time as a trainer. She is also a certified yoga instructor. Cally resides in St. Louis with her husband, best friend, and travel partner, Rich, and their very outspoken dog, Scout. She never went back to school but isn't ruling it out. She is only twenty-six after all.

www.facebook.com/cally.rolwes
www.instagram.com/callyfornia_dreamin/

ERIC ROSEN

I Taught Myself

The amount of life you feel is directly proportionate to your willingness to face the fears that threaten your dreams.

— Richard Rudd

When I was a child, I would wake up excited to see what new adventure would unfold. I loved seeing the sunrise. I didn't care about an agenda or the time of the day. It was the spaces between what my mom had planned that I looked forward to. Even when she would go shopping, I would hide in the center of the circular clothes racks, pretending I was in the Batcave.

I was devastated by my parents' divorce. I thought it was my fault Mom left because I expressed a wide range of emotions. *I taught myself it wasn't OK to be a sensitive kid.*

Gazing out the windows, waiting for her to come home, I would close my eyes and see colors, shapes, and objects. I had no idea what they meant, but *I taught myself not to tell anyone what I could see.*

I went to summer school after kindergarten, probably because I had a hard time paying attention in class after the divorce. One day I was scribbling with joy, shading a picture of a pig with a black crayon, refusing to color between the lines. My teacher snatched the paper and exclaimed, "I don't like the way you are coloring!" WTF. *I taught myself it's not OK to color outside the lines or express intensity, and I better figure out what is going on at all times.*

By age eleven, living with my dad had taken its toll on me. His erratic outbursts when I asked curious questions had me constantly wary. *I taught myself to be overly cautious about how I talk to people, so I don't offend them.*

Ages eleven to sixteen were painfully innocuous. My mascot would have been Eeyore from Winnie the Pooh. Woe was me, teased about everything, from the way I dressed to being skinny. *I taught myself to blend in.*

Age seventeen, I got my first girlfriend. My sense of value increased. I felt validated. At twenty-two, I was at the peak of my game. I had seniority in my fraternity, had signed the biggest salary of any recent graduate (among my friends), and was dating the girl I planned to marry. *I taught myself external validation felt damn good.*

The rest of my twenties were a treacherous decline. The relationship crashed and burned, leaving me a single father. My life derailed far from the tracks of my expectations. I'd replay things in my head, like my son's mother describing me as "so affectionate" and "sensitive." She wasn't complimenting me. I reminded myself of the lesson from Mom's departure: *expressing love just puts you at risk of heartbreak.*

At the bar on my twenty-seventh birthday, I'm drunkenly slumped over, my head hanging low. My friend asks, "What happened to you, man? You used to walk around like you owned the place!" He was right. I'd officially lost my confidence.

One day I came home carrying twelve bags of groceries in one hand and my eighteen-month-old son in the other. I slumped to the floor with the bags and my toddler and acknowledged I couldn't manage ten-hour days, parenting, and my health much longer. But I didn't see a way out. *I taught myself that until this changes, I just have to get it done.*

I prayed to get out of this cycle. The universe answered my prayers. I was laid off at work and there was a fire in the house. I'd spend the next few years diving into a self-development journey to make myself "better," since all my life *I'd taught myself there was something wrong with me.*

This path eventually led me to become a spiritual seeker. I found comfort in things like Reiki, Astrology, and Ayahuasca ceremonies. I experienced a spiritual awakening and an awareness of things I couldn't previously explain, like the colors and shapes I used to see as a kid now taking the form of visions connected to emotions. I found a bridge to my psychic abilities.

Surrounded by a community of like-minded friends all over the St. Louis region, I began to feel confident about myself. With an arsenal of tools at my disposal, from nutritional guidance to spiritual insight, I started my own coaching business and began filming daily Facebook Live videos because I had so many creative concepts I wanted to share with everyone!

Business wasn't building the way I had hoped, even after a few years. I had a lot of self-doubt and would retreat from my work. My expression on video was often rigid. My viewers noticed. Many of my spiritual friendships dissolved, and it was just me, my son, and my shadow. Because I felt unworthy, I was comfortable hiding from people. This backward step got my attention. I was carrying a decade of heavy financial and romantic losses, trying to help everyone else on social media, and launching multiple failed ideas. I did whatever I could to avoid giving myself self-love, acceptance, a makeover of my self-concept, and elimination of fear-based beliefs.

After suffering a complete mental breakdown while camping in the Arizona desert, I came face-to-face with the little doorway in *Alice in Wonderland* and found the *shift* I needed. I opened the door with acceptance. I was ready to take responsibility, starting with the pain I had caused my loved ones by not loving myself. I had treated those closest to me the way I treated myself. I'd been dancing and dodging around truths and was afraid to slow down long enough to face the fears covering up those truths.

In my own real-life movie, I played the martyr, the victim, the saboteur, and the underachiever. All of these diabolical nasties caused mental and emotional chaos within and around me, as evidenced by my crippled finances, strained relationships, and sinking business.

My trauma-fueled stories of inadequacy, *all those things I taught myself,* dictated the trajectory of my life. They were all designed to keep me from facing my ultimate trepidation: *owning my power.*

After deciding to return to the Midwest, I made a pact with myself, which I renew daily—especially when shame tries to launch a sneak attack to undermine my momentum. My commitments are to:

24

- Create and read my life vision statement every day
- Act from a place of inspiration and desire
- Have compassion for my actions and creativity
- Focus on self-love and acceptance
- Slow down
- Self-validate

I affirm these commitments to myself with grace. The only way I know I can grow is through play, kindness, creativity, and love. These are my allies and core values. After years of teaching myself how to hide and survive, I began to reeducate myself. I've taught myself:

- It's great to express emotions.
- I'm allowed to trigger people with how I speak if it's not my intention to offend.
- It's OK to stand out from the crowd.
- Self-validation is the only validation that matters.
- Expressing love in spite of its perceived risk is courageous.
- Confidence can always be rebuilt.
- I get to choose to do only what I love.
- There was never anything wrong with me.

The more I surrendered to and focused on the things I wanted in my life, the more opportunities started showing up. I was blessed by many beautiful souls who came to support me. The relationship with my son began to blossom. Our interactions were more fluid and compassionate. I joined men's groups and reignited my own passion and style for mentoring other men. I accepted a deepening sense of internal peace.

The vision I have for my life is to go on the adventure. I feel most aligned when I'm intentionally saying yes to challenges, treating them like theater, choreographing a joyful dance of freedom with whatever life throws at me. Every moment feels best when I recognize it as an opportunity for my soul to grow.

I've spent enough time with my triggers of inadequacy to know my true calling is to play, innocently, without shame, embarking into the unknown to follow my dreams. You won't find me hiding in clothes racks anymore. You'll find me sharing the good news I've found through all I've learned, especially coaching men, showing them it is safe to be who we are, emotions and all. It's OK to slow down and be a *compassionate steward* of what already exists in the world. There is no goal or any person that needs to be chased, especially those that threaten our vitality. There is no one to save, except maybe our own creative innocence. Having faith in a better, more loving world than the one we stepped into is key, as well as practicing our own unique roles in advancing that dream forward. Our inner child, our relationships, all our children and their children's children will all celebrate our strength and build on it for generations to come.

Eric Rosen has always been highly motivated and ambitious. Upon becoming a young single father, he began to see that much of his goal orientation in life was motivated by the shame of not being good enough. Once he realized he didn't have to prove anything to anyone, he authentically began expressing himself in ways he could only imagine before. With a decade of dedicated soul-searching and service to others, Eric aspires to share the insights he has learned to help others along their journey of finding community in life. A Men's Coach, Astrologer, and shaman, Eric speaks publicly to inspire men to free themselves from the emotional constraints of shame and to pursue true purpose and passion in life. He facilitates 1:1 coaching sessions, group coaching, and workshops for guys who are looking to courageously overcome perceived limitations of the mind.

linktr.ee/vikingrisingmenscoach

BILL STRINGER

From Playground Games to Wholeness: Men Hurt and Heal Too!

Most people consider me kindhearted, generous, resourceful, intelligent, successful. I don't recall ever being referred to as insecure or unstable…until someone did.

Growing up in a small town one hour south of St. Louis, Missouri, offered an escape to a five-year-old boy from the potential harms of the inner-city school ground games. It also offered growth and creativity! I recall every day of that life—whether it was one of the hot, humid summer days or one of the cold, snowy days—as being an adventure. Country kids can make anything into a game. You name it! Rocks for balls, sticks for bats, scrap wood for clubhouses, boxes and extra blankets for hideouts, using word of mouth to gather together a good football, kickball, or baseball game, cardboard for replica stadiums, Atari for overnight sleepovers, plastic bags for sleds. Even when times were tough, we made a meal out of lettuce, radishes, tomatoes, cheese, celery, cucumbers! Whatever our lot, we made something out of nothing. We were Huckleberry Fin turned Rachael Ray! I never would have imagined playground games would come back to visit me as a forty-four-year-old man, but they did!

The Seduction

It was a warm, late summer/early fall day. I had been corresponding with her on Match.com for just over a month, off and on, one- or two-line messages. I finally broke through for a date. Her coy "catch me if you can" vibes came through the app so powerfully, my hunt-and-conquer-manly-appetite was awakened. Two years removed from a loveless marriage, I was ready to give my all in this newly found playground of love. She was so beautiful. Her scent took me back into the fields where anything was possible. The way she would look at me made me feel like I could do or be anything. Simply put, her look and touch made me melt like M&M's on a hot Southeastern Missouri summer day. She was confident and mysterious. I was smitten. Intoxicated.

Our early conversations were exhilarating, even though they inevitably included something about her ex, how he couldn't measure up. And how other white men she'd dated were "like watching paint dry." She stroked my ego, and I felt increasingly strong, worthy, like I was special, the best.

Then things began to change. It was subtle, yet profound. I started to feel like what I now describe as putting change into an empty vending machine. I ignored the signs that said, "Out of Order" and was determined to get something out of it.

What drove me to keep putting change in the machine? Hearing the words, "No one has ever made me feel like you do. You're the love of my life." Love bombing would always be mixed in with disrespect and put-downs (intermittent reinforcement), making me feel less than a man. Lies and manipulation caused me to doubt my own reality. I'd question her, and she would say, "I never said that. You're imagining things."

It was pure torment and torture, a "pull me in, push me away" strategy that became the catalyst for a what I now call her "soul vampire destruction project."

I was in a toxic, dangerous relationship, a transaction, an exchange of my good for her evil. I felt as vulnerable as if I were a cast member on the show *Naked and Afraid*. I didn't know what to do but realized there was no reasoning with evil. The only thing left for me was to remove myself from what I loved, which was the hardest thing I ever had to do in my life. The torment and torture continued.

Growing up in a small town and open fields, with life an adventure, I didn't know anything about what I was experiencing. To survive this, I had to think like a survivor, setting aside all emotions. Logic and black-and-white decision-making replaced feelings, allowing me to make the hardest decision in my life. I decided to change the locks and file a restraining order and *never* speak to her again. It was the only way to survival and healing!

Lessons Learned: From Destruction to Wholeness

As men, our society has unrightfully taught us to not be vulnerable, to hold it in, not to cry but to deal with it! The truth is men are vulnerable and have feelings.

Toxic people come in all shapes and disguises. They may be beautiful and offer adventure, but toxic is not normal. Emotional and psychological abuse is not normal. It's destructive. Before I realized it, goodness, kindness, generosity, sanity, and innocence had been sucked out of me in exchange for someone else's pain, shame, bitterness, and pure evil. It was parasitical, like a scavenger consuming my soul. I had to get out!

In October of 2020, the day of my trial from a one-year marriage (yes, an actual court trial), I admitted myself into the hospital to be treated for stress-induced diverticulitis. My colon and bladder were tying together. Later, I suffered significant back issues, including arthritis (which can be incited by bowel issues), and eventually had a partial colectomy.

My mind and my heart could not accept what was happening. My ego tried to hide, to stay in denial and disbelief, but my body would not allow it. It fought back by making me ill.

Kitchen Work

My healing began in the kitchen (which is another book). I see the kitchen as a place to nourish and be nourished, to make stuff out of otherwise useless stand-alone ingredients. It's a place to be creative, to turn something that looks worthless or ugly into something beautiful.

I restored my heart-sick soul and healed my self-destroying body by discovering how to nourish first my body, then my mind. I rediscovered the ten-year-old that made delicious tomato and cucumber sandwiches, making something from nothing.

They say time heals all wounds. I have friends who years after a toxic or traumatic experience remain bitter, sick and in no way healed.

My approach: *Hard work*! Here's what to do:

1. Listen to your body
2. Recognize the five stages of healing and grief:
   a. Denial
   b. Anger
   c. Bargaining
   d. Depression
   e. Acceptance
6. Be creative
   a. Do the "unthinkable"—take a walk, go for a run, or ride a bike to places you've never been
   b. Carry through with bucket-list items that take you out of your comfort zone
3. Enlist a support network—those that listen, don't judge, and have your interests at heart
4. Find a counselor who understands toxic abuse
5. Read a lot, especially books on abuse and healing
6. Pray and meditate. If you don't know how to enter into a meditative state, research the topic and/or find a qualified energy healer or counselor
7. Try energy healing. I never believed in this until I tried it. Much needed!
8. Don't move too quickly into another relationship; honor the process of healing
9. Allow yourself to feel pain; learn to visualize healing
   a. Cry, yes cry
   b. Mourn
   c. Absorb and release
   d. Talk it through as much as you need to
   e. Accept
   f. Quietly celebrate the good

Rebuilding

My shift has been painful, as they often are. I learned that abuse is abuse. It's not about someone else being crazy. Narcissistic abuse is specific, and it's very destructive. Learn about it. Learn from it! Study it. Escape it! Become a better you because of it! Your life depends on it.

Finally, every day, follow these ten rebuilding steps that I journaled on a plane ride in October 2021:

1. Pray and/or meditate daily
2. Read at least one self-help book per month
3. Take your power back by not giving it away; invest in your self-worth
4. Get to know the other person in a relationship. See them for who they are, set boundaries, and stop focusing on how they're making you feel
5. Master the art of *shifting the monkey*[1]
6. Eat better (cut sweets and pastries, reduce intake) and lose thirty pounds
7. Exercise at least three times a week
8. Eliminate behaviors that cause emotional and physical vulnerabilities
9. Stay focused on life goals (business development, income alternatives, rental properties, life-coaching launch)
10. Address conflict resolution vulnerabilities by confronting issues, creating healthy boundaries, accepting others' responses while not absorbing them, taking responsibility where merited, making decisions, and not looking back.

I have one final recommendation. Remember what it feels like to play, to nourish the little kid inside yourself who just wants to have an adventure.

Bill Stringer has spent seventeen years as a finance professional with Toyota and Lexus and is a vacation home Superhost on Airbnb and Vrbo. Born in St. Louis and raised in Southeast Missouri, Bill's path took him to college where he graduated with a degree in music performance at Welch College in Nashville, Tennessee. He then spent eight years in full-time ministry as a worship pastor where he experienced and developed what he calls foundational passion and experience in helping others. He also wrote several worship songs. Bill is currently launching his Life Coaching business, *NextLife Coaching*, which focuses on helping men understand that being vulnerable is OK. His passion is to help his clients become a better version of themselves through self-awareness, pain transformation, and healing into wholeness.

1 *Shifting the Monkey* by Todd Whitaker **discloses the art of protecting good people from liars, criers, and other slackers**. Whitaker defines "monkeys" as the responsibilities, obligations, and problems that everyone carries and deals with every day, but that often get shifted to someone else.

Trials to Triumphs

Insecure. Low self-esteem. Avoiding the desire that was inside.

That is who I was until about 2012 when a major shift happened "for" me. I was faced with a totally unexpected divorce that would lead me toward living my best life!

In 2012, when the divorce happened, I didn't think my life could ever be OK again. My emotions plummeted as I struggled to revive a marriage that ended suddenly. I had been a stay-at-home mom for thirteen years and married for almost sixteen years. I loved taking care of my family and had happily put aside my goals to be a wife and homemaker. It was important to me. It was all I knew.

I was terrified and felt helpless. It seemed all I could do was worry, and boy did I worry: how it would affect my kids' lives, if I would lose friends, what were people thinking, and the worst, how I would support myself and the kids. The wind was knocked out of me.

These feelings were compounded by the insecurities I had buried for years. I was always second-guessing everything! Hoping for the best. I could finally see how my insecurities caused me to ignore the red flags in my marriage.

I had no income at this time and was totally unprepared to begin a career. My biggest concern was how to make my children feel as safe and comfortable as possible. For a while, I kept hoping I could save my marriage. I was a fighter, especially for my family, but I had no clue the marriage was unsalvageable.

I kept asking myself, "How did I end up here? Why me?" There was no communication, which made it impossible to get any answers to why this choice was made *for* me.

Everyone was in shock, even our immediate families. I felt like someone died. I was experiencing so many feelings, and I was scared to admit that it was really happening. Again with the worries: what were my kids going through as they had to tell their friends, how to pay for things, who would judge me, were people laughing or talking behind my back, what's wrong with me, why did this happen. I was focused on all the wrong things, but that is how I'd always coped. I was insecure. I felt like I couldn't make a decision or take a step without overthinking or asking for advice. I cried myself to sleep, then put on a strong face to make it through the day. After about two months of pleading to save what we had, I finally admitted that wasn't going to happen. Accepting the end of the relationship I'd built my life around was the only way I could go forward.

Where was I going to start now? I had put aside any thought of my career or goals to take care of my family. Then it hit me. "In what way is giving up one's dreams or passion ever good?"

I have always believed each of us has a special gift, a purpose that will impact others. I wanted to find that gift inside me. I had so much to give but wasn't sure where to focus.

That's when I started leaning on my faith, hit my knees, and prayed that God would give me answers. I also prayed for strength to show my kids everything would be OK and to be able to provide the support and love they needed. I was determined I would not let this hold my children or myself back in any way!

When I started to pray, God showed up in the amazing ways that God does. I began to feel God's comfort, letting me know I didn't have to worry, that I would be OK, my children would be OK, and we would make it through this.

I started to see precious miracles through the kindness of complete strangers in the craziest places. I would look up and say "Thank you, God. I know that was from you!" One instance was when I was shopping at Sam's Club. I was in a hurry, wanting to get in and get out. I don't remember what happened to me that morning, but something with the divorce had me upset. I was upset a lot. Sadly, this was just another one of those days.

As I was walking out, a lady came over to me and said, "I wanted to approach you in the store, but I didn't want to seem weird." She was sweet and complimentary. Then she finally said, "You need to know that everything is going to be okay. I couldn't miss the chance to say that to you."

I immediately got butterflies, and a sense of calmness came over me. Her encouraging words helped me shift my fears to hopes. I thanked her, and we even hugged. As soon as I got in my car, I cried, looked up, and said, "Thank you God, I know that was you letting me know it will be OK."

This would happen to me in the most random places—even the airport one time! After this had happened several times, I promised myself I would never miss an opportunity to be kind to someone or to show support for others. These strangers had no idea what I was going through but went out of their way to show me kindness, and it would completely change the course of my day! Leading me to the SHIFT I needed!

Through the intense chaos of the divorce, my thoughts began to change. I surrounded myself with family and supportive friends. I changed my focus. I began going out, doing things I'd always wanted to do, even though I never felt ready. I knew I had to do these things whether I was ready or not. I had to work through the lack of confidence and step out in faith.

Fitness and real estate are two things I have always loved. I decided to get my real estate license, and, in the meantime, I started competing in area fitness competitions. Placing in the top three standings in my first competition gave me the desire to keep competing. In the next two competitions, I placed in the top two standings, which qualified me to compete at the national level. These competitions were a huge blessing in my life at this time. Competing taught me to work through my fears and insecurities, kept my focus positive, showed me strength and determination I never knew I had. I was enjoying life, forming life-long friendships and connections while learning to live through the chaos going on around me!

My shift unfolded in front of me. I saw how I could move forward with determination and faith, even through adversity, to break through the dark times! I was finally WINNING at life and for my kids!

Many of the connections I made during competitions also helped with my real estate career. Putting the fear aside helped me form incredible relationships. I started networking and made important connections that were integral to my success. Working in real estate allowed me to collaborate with incredible people and form unique bonds with clients who have impacted my life in special ways. Now I accept that with each client, we are meant to help each other!

My new mantras: "Be a warrior, not a worrier. Never be ashamed to share my story. Encourage others to share their story about how they've overcome challenges."

We all have a story. Someone needs to hear your story. It could be the story that helps them with their breakthrough.

My story is still unfolding. I'm still learning how to get through challenges as they come. I know that to overcome my fears I have to shift my focus, stay in faith, and be intentional with my thoughts. I am grateful to have the support of my kids in this journey. I've felt their love and encouragement every step of the way. My greatest accomplishment is being their mom, and having them cheer me on while achieving my goals means everything to me!

My purpose now is to inspire others to follow their dreams, regardless of how dim, twisted, or uncertain the path. We need to move forward regardless of the dark times. That's the only way to emerge in the light. If we don't risk, we can't gain. We grow through the hard times, not the easy times.

Never let a setback hold you back. Shift your thoughts and actions, and be intentional with how you want to move through adversities. Remember there is no testimony without a test. I'm not saying to ignore the negative thoughts or feelings. Acknowledge your feelings, take time to process them, and have a support system and plan in place that directs you out of adversity. Learn to step up, even when you are scared. Start living your best life. You have a gift that will impact the lives of others!

Tina Knox is an entrepreneur, fitness enthusiast, mother of two amazing children, Blake & Hannah, married to her best friend, Jeremy Knox, and is now a contributing author. Tina has been a licensed real estate agent in Missouri since 2012, advising clients in residential, commercial, land and distressed sales. Collaborating directly with buyers, sellers, builders, relocation services, investors, and attorneys, she is determined to give each client top-notch service. She is a member of the St. Louis and St. Charles Association of Realtors, Women's Council of Realtors, and she was awarded STL Agent of the Year in 2020 (*St. Louis Magazine*) and has been on HGTV's *House Hunters* twice! Tina supports Second Chance Ranch, a community charity organization, by donating from each closing. She loves staying active with family, friends, and her two dogs.

Connect with Tina via email at tina@knoxproperties.net or one of the following:
www.facebook.com/realtorstl
www.knoxproperties.net
www.instagram.com/tinaknox_realestate/

Dancing with Grief

*I leaned over my bed to look at my phone for what seemed like the
hundredth time. 3:00 a.m. and, still, sleep escaped me.*

My brain was trying to take in all the events that had transpired over the last twenty-four hours. Just twelve hours earlier, I was sitting at my husband's bedside, holding his hand and telling him goodbye. Telling him it was all right to leave all the pain and suffering that cancer had brought to his life over the past four years.

I had envisioned a goodbye like you see in the movies, being able to have a heartfelt conversation where we could share our love for each other one more time, one last time. Unfortunately, Jeff was in a very deep sleep and was unresponsive. I pleaded with God to wake him up—just for a moment—so I could look into his blue eyes one more time and see that slight smirk on his face that always made me smile inside and out, to lock eyes and connect like we had hundreds of times before in our day-to-day interactions. But Jeff was already starting to drift away. His hospice doctor had just shared with me the importance of giving him permission to die. It sounded crazy at the time. My brain was still grappling with the nightmare I was living. But she was right. Approximately six hours after I tearfully and lovingly told my husband that I loved him more than words could say, thanked him for being a part of my life for this season, that I would eventually get my footing back, and our family and friends would take good care of me, he took his last breath and very peacefully entered into eternity.

Those last moments of his physical life here on Earth, while the most painful, also contained so much beauty and love. Knowing that I got to be with this precious man as his journey came to an end and observe the peacefulness that swept over him (and surprisingly even over me) was and will be a gift I will treasure forever.

So, what now? How was I supposed to live this life without my partner, my best friend, my confidante, my sounding board, *my person*? I had lived a caretaker life for almost four years since the "C" word had entered our vocabulary and become a day-to-day reality in our lives. Who was I supposed to be now? I was no longer a wife, nurse, cook, secretary, driver, whatever. In just one moment, I was now a widow. My husband was gone, and I had to figure out all the next steps in life alone. That's the tricky thing I learned about grief. It wasn't just losing *my* person and painfully missing his physical presence, but I lost a piece of myself in the process.

I was very blessed to have met my soulmate through the wonderful world of the internet. An algorithm on a giant computer matched me to him, him to me. While we had both been hurt by relationships in the past, thankfully we sought out love at the same time. Our lives were forever changed after the first messages were exchanged. Three years of dating and a six-hundred-mile move later, we were husband and wife. A year after the wedding, we plunged into working full time together in the company Jeff had started eight years before we met. Living together, working together, doing life together. It had potential for disaster, but thankfully it was quite the opposite.

We were a good match from the start, and we complemented each other as much professionally as we did personally. But that time came to an end just eleven short years after we said, "I do." *How* did that happen? I couldn't help feeling there had been a serious mistake in the grand plan for me to be without my love already.

I never truly understood loss and grief until after I said goodbye to my sweet Jeffrey. Before this, I naively thought the death of someone was just a horrible event that over time you *get over*, you move on, you meet someone else, and *boom*—your grief is healed. I chuckle just writing that out and reading it aloud. If only it were that simple!

I equate the grief process to a dance. An even better descriptor would be of a *dance partner*. At the beginning, grief was just dragging me around on the dance floor. I really had no idea what steps I was taking, what music was playing, and where I was half the time.

I know that Jeff is probably looking down and laughing at me writing about dancing. I'm a horrible dancer! I grew up in the *Footloose* home, like the movie. No dancing, no rock music. He, on the other hand, grew up with a family who hosted weekly disco parties in their garage. He was always the leader on the dance floor when it came to the two of us, and he even convinced me to learn the Thriller dance when we were on a cruise.

The fog of initial grief is real and relentless. To the outside world, it may have appeared that I was rebounding just fine. It truly was not the case. I don't remember a lot of details the few months after Jeff's death. I had an amazing tribe of family and friends who helped me when I was going through the motions of regular and normal life. It felt as if I were watching myself from afar. Those people filled in the gaps in so many ways, as I literally didn't have the mental bandwidth to accomplish even the smallest tasks.

While physical dancing is not my thing (or at least not yet), I have learned how to dance with grief over the last twenty months and will continue to do so throughout the rest of my life. Grief is something that will be part of my life forever now. After working with a therapist, I've learned to leave space for the sadness that sweeps over me when I remember and realize Jeff will never again be by my side, this side of heaven. I'm able to be vulnerable enough to cry in front of people, and I know releasing sorrow will help me heal and be a better person. I am certain I am more able to empathize with others who have also encountered a great loss in their lives.

Grief is the reminder that I loved Jeff deeply, and as weird as it sounds, I'm grateful for this grief as it shows the deep love we shared in the brief season we had together. Grief is dancing with memories, both good and bad. It's remembering Jeff's body painfully falling apart after a final surgery confirmed his cancer was no longer treatable. It's having thoughts of regret for not taking advantage of the time I had left with him to have close, intimate, and meaningful conversations. Instead, I kept myself busy with the tasks of caretaking. That was easier than giving up hope and trying to imagine my life without him by my side. Some memories I dance with make me smile and laugh. Memories of Corvette rides, scorpion hunting, and nuzzling into the crook of his neck where I fit perfectly when we hugged. (I called it my nook.) Sometimes the dance shifts to a future grief where I am sad for all the things that we won't get to experience together. The trips we won't get to take, the business we won't be able to watch grow, the growth we won't see in each other and in our marriage. There is no more future with my husband, just the past. Memories are irreplaceable. While they cannot replace the loss, they are a comfort and provide a connection back to my sweet husband.

While executing my complicated dance with grief, I am slowly learning to give myself grace and have gratitude for the person I am now. Acknowledging that while I'll never be the same dance partner as I was with Jeff, and that there will always be a spot of sadness in my life without him, I have much to look forward to in this life I have left to live. I have a purpose in creating a different future, my future. I can honor Jeff in how I live each day. More importantly, I can honor myself and the wonderful way God created me.

I will take bold, brave, imperfect steps on a dance floor made of love and contribution. While I'm dancing, I will refine my steps, knowing there will always be a few tricky ones. I will need to keep practicing so each movement helps me get my footing for the next season God brings my way. And although I may not be a skilled dancer, I can help teach others how to dance with grief and find joy.

Kimberly Schilling is an entrepreneur and owner of Creative Works, an industry-leading company that creates memorable experiences through immersive, live-based entertainment attractions. Kimberly and her husband, Jeff, have been featured in several entertainment industry publications and recognized for innovation and creativity within the family entertainment industry. With a background in education, Kimberly was instrumental in creating a business program for entrepreneurs in the attraction business that teaches best practices, design, and marketing. She has been involved with projects providing memorable environments, unique décor, and props for the Make-a-Wish Foundation, Extreme Home Makeover, and multiple faith-based organizations. To honor her late husband, Kimberly is founding Rise Up from the Ashes, a nonprofit that will give back to others who are striving to rise above life's difficulties. She is a proud "Auntie" to five nieces and nephews, and a mom to a fur baby, Bentley.

www.thewoweffect.com
kimberly@riseupfromtheashes.org
www.facebook.com/kimbatoast
www.linkedin.com/in/kimberly-schilling-4867a628/

MATTHEW MUSHLIN

Can You Hear Me?

When he was six years old, his mom told him,
"If God would let you, you would talk twenty-four hours a day!"
So, he did.

Conversations flowed effortlessly for him, and he was passionately interested in the fiber of those conversations, which led to a lifetime of cherished relationships.

For thirty years, he was in sales in international finance, insurance, college and retirement planning. Then it was time for a new chapter, this time in real estate! Within eight months, he was on the road to being Rookie of the Year in his new career.

Then, in September 2019, things started happening. The first big one was when he was driving to his office. Someone hit him going 52-mph in a 35-mph zone, totaling a perfect Benz SUV and putting him in the hospital for two days. Accidents happen.

In October, he went on a trip with his wife and friends, which started out great and ended terribly. So terribly, she sat him down when they got home to tell him she wanted a separation. A week later, she'd moved out and taken his twelve-year-old dog with her.

This was *never* part of his life plan. The loss of his twenty-year marriage consumed him. Then, in November, his business partner decided to go on her own because she couldn't deal with the personal bullshit he was going through and she was tired of hearing about it.

In December, he was on a business trip and received a phone call from the wife of his dearest friend of thirty-seven years telling him he'd just passed away.

Sure, he'd known his friend was sick, but he didn't know he was *that* sick. He never had a chance to say goodbye. Overwhelmed with grief, he collapsed at the entrance to his hotel, and a bellman helped him to his room.

Things kept happening.

His beloved dog developed breathing problems. Remember, this guy is separated from his wife. They share the dog each week. She took him to the vet, but she was out of town on business when the test results came back. The dog had congestive heart failure.

He called his wife and told her, "Roscoe could live a year, or a week. He could pass at any time."

His wife, in tears, said, "You know what, we've got to put our stuff aside. You're moving in with me and we're going to love this dog together for however long he has! Pack your bag. I'll be back tonight!"

He did. He wanted to work on the marriage and thought being together would help, until she came home from a business trip and found a pot in the sink that he forgot to wash, again. He got up to wash it and then put it away, hoping to go back to their evening. She wasn't done being upset.

"I think you should leave," she told him.

"Are you serious?" he asked.

She said "Yes!" and he left.

The next day, he called a friend to take him to the airport to go to the memorial for his best friend. While he was at the memorial, his wife called.

"The therapist thinks we shouldn't see each other anymore except to exchange the dog, and our conversations should only be about the dog." That limiting!

Then came the really big one no one was expecting: a global pandemic. During the shutdown, the marriage counselor had them write each other letters.

It's May 2020. His wife called and asked if they could get together to read their letters to each other. He let her read first.

"We did all we could," she read, "but I don't see any way of making this marriage work. I want a friendly divorce. We will always be family."

He didn't bother to read his letter. She wanted to hear what he wrote, but there was no point. She'd made the decision. For both of them.

He stood and said, "You've been a great wife. I'm sorry for my part in this. I'll need time to process what's just happened."

It wasn't just the end of the marriage. He realized she'd made 95 percent of the decisions during their marriage. He *let* her make the decisions. This time was no different. But with that knowledge sinking in, his awareness began to shift. He began to hear a new voice in his head, but the message was unclear.

In July 2020 he called his doctor, who referred him to a specialist, and within ten minutes the specialist said, without hesitation, "Go downstairs and get a biopsy immediately. I think you have cancer."

The guy sat there, a million thoughts racing through his head. *Cancer?*

"Okay, how do we fix this?" he asked. "I've got a life to live!" Worrying was never how he processed, and he wasn't going to start then.

January 15, 2021, he got a nagging sore throat that wouldn't go away. He talked for a living. This had happened before, but never to this degree.

The next step was a tracheostomy with a month-long stay in the hospital, followed by speech and physical therapy.

He couldn't work. The dog was with the wife. He really missed his dog, whose breathing condition kept getting worse, but he didn't realize how bad until his wife called at 1:08 a.m. to tell him that his dog only had minutes left. She thought he should know. She had been at the vet for two hours but waited to call, making it impossible for him to be there at the end.

About twenty minutes later, he read her simple text, "He's gone." He didn't get to say goodbye.

Just when he thought things couldn't get any worse, the cancer returned. It's September and a second tracheostomy is performed, again requiring another month-long stay in the hospital.

The sore throat returned in October. The cancer had come back. Again, he thought for thirty seconds and said, "Let's do whatever we've got to do. I've got a life to live!"

That led to a complete laryngectomy, which meant he lost his vocal cords, the most extreme outcome he had feared from the onset.

This guy, who'd spent his entire life speaking for a living to help others achieve their goals and dreams, was now a *laryngectomee*. His only communication was typing on a smartphone or over email.

This guy is me.

I can't make a living, my wife wants a divorce, my dog has passed, and during a global pandemic, I had three bouts of cancer. I became, quite literally, speechless. However, my listening improved.

My epiphany was realizing that even when I was able to talk, I was not heard. Now I can't talk quite yet, but I can listen. And listening has allowed me to discover another voice inside of me. That voice reminds me that while I may have very little control over winning or losing, I can control how I play the game.

Finally, I now believe that everything *does* happen for a reason. It's just not always in the plan. So, what do I do?

Before cancer, I was a big talker. I've been told I was a good listener. Friends told me I was a joy to have a conversation with, that I was empathetic. This was true. I believe it will be true again.

I smile. Every day.

My posts on social media are intended to inspire others to never, ever let go of hope or faith for a brighter tomorrow.

I'd like to blame other people and circumstances on the negative things that have happened to me, but I wasn't the narrator. I performed the lead role in this whole disaster.

Far from quitting, I'm beginning. I accept that my life is my responsibility. My choice is to become my best, most authentic self. Finally listening to myself, I hear the voice that speaks to my soul. My purpose is to give this new voice every opportunity to share words I never knew before, and for those words to be healing. Knowing I have things to say that may never be heard, I'm going to learn from this pain that is difficult to explain and help others be heard. Because as I have learned that the quieter you become, the more you learn.

Matthew Mushlin entered The Art Institute of Fort Lauderdale at sixteen years old with love for the human spirit, a natural ability to connect with others, a desire to explore the world, and a passion for fine arts. He photographed celebrities such as Elle Macpherson and Meg Ryan and conducted travel shoots in exotic locations such as Miami, Florida, and Okinawa, Japan. Through his travels, Matthew found challenges, growth, and excitement, which guided him through a thirty-five-year career across many industries in international sales, finance, and consulting. His work relationships included mom-and-pop local shops, entrepreneurial boutiques, Fortune 500, Fortune 100, and publicly traded companies. Matthew's desire to create lasting, successful partnerships, his love of people, and his drive to "close the deal" transitioned his career into real estate in 2018. Licensed in North Carolina and Missouri, he developed SellMeStLouis.com, a unique branding strategy to help pair amazing people with their dream homes.

matthewmushlin007@gmail.com
www.facebook.com/matthew.mushlin
www.facebook.com/SellMeStLouis/
www.instagram.com/matthewmuchfun/
www.instagram.com/sellmestlouis/

Hopium

Your addiction to Hopium is costing you your dreams.

How often do you use the word "hope" in your life? What if I told you that single word may be the exact reason you aren't getting the things you desire most in your life? You might be thinking, "Wait a second, hope isn't a bad thing!" Keep reading and I'll explain why this seemingly benign word should be eradicated from your vocabulary, and *if* you intentionally execute what you learn in this chapter, you will transform your life.

Before we continue, why should you listen to me? Who am I to be spouting advice? My experience includes fourteen different start-up companies, scaling and growing SaaS and service-based businesses. I have been happily married for eighteen years, and together we are raising two teenagers. In addition to being a lifelong student, I've dedicated over six years to deep personal growth, both physical and emotional. Each of these by themselves feel like monumental achievements that I'm very proud of, but I've got to be honest with you, I'm far behind where I planned to be!

So why is that? The answer is "hope." Where does this word show up in your life? If you are like me, maybe it came from "trusting the universe" or "trusting the divine." After some deep reflection, I've come to the conclusion that hope is another word for "giving up responsibility." Let that resonate for a minute . . .

The purpose of this chapter is to give you an understanding of how powerful language is, and to provide a simple exercise you can use to get laser-focused on how to actualize what is truly important to you.

To be clear, I'm incredibly grateful for who and where I am in life, but I want more. If you are reading this, I assume you are also looking to improve some facet of your life. It's not just about more money in the bank; I want to give more, I want to teach more, I want to love more, and I want to serve more. In order to do all of these things, I first need to *be* more. To be crystal clear, I need to "Be More Intentional!"

Ready to dive in? Let's go.

First, let's start with the definition: *Hopium* is the belief that a situation will somehow work itself out in our favor.

Presently, we exist in a time of "manifesting reality," "quantum meditation," and "willing things to happen." Given all that, why is hope such a bad thing? Remember this, the words we use every day have a massive effect on our thoughts and, more importantly, on our actions. *When we use the word "hope," we are essentially abdicating the responsibility of taking action.* Read that again.

Consider this example: you want to improve your relationship, so you think and/or express out loud: *I hope our marriage works out.*

Now ask yourself, does saying this make you feel like you are ready to put your full energy into creating a magical experience for yourself and your partner? Probably not.

Let's convert that objective to be intentional: *I'm going to calendar at least two hours every week to work on my relationship. I'll use books/podcasts/mentors to gain knowledge. We will go out on more date nights, and with that new knowledge we've gained, we'll create more excitement and fun in our relationship.* Sounds a bit different, right? And more importantly, it *feels* different. Remember, we aren't really after the outcomes; we are all chasing the feelings the outcomes give us. Our chase requires that the words we use every day, what we focus our attention on, and the actions we take *intentionally* drive us toward that feeling.

[Visualize the feeling you are after and take action to get closer your Oasis.]

How can we be more intentional about the things we really want? Within this brief chapter, I'm going to show you how you can quickly shift from being hopeful to becoming intentional. I'm providing examples that I trust all entrepreneurs and business folks will be able to relate to, and I'll include strategies to overcome our addiction to Hopium. In order to reach the next level, you must have the courage to take the first step. Think: crawl, walk, run, sprint.

"I hope this deal works out."

Over the past several years, I've been working on an automation platform to simplify the sales and marketing process in order to stay top of mind, create raving fans, and drive new revenue. Because I've been a part of, or advised, the technology and operations departments of many different companies, I'm in the unique position of truly understanding the needs of almost any business simply by asking a few questions.

In one of my businesses, we were in desperate need to improve the way we stay top of mind and consistently follow up with our prospects, clients, and partners. We've all heard that "the fortune is in the follow-up." While this isn't a ground-breaking discovery, why is it that I have yet to work with a business that has nailed the follow-up process? The short answer is lack of resources: lack of capable staff, lack of systems and processes, or lack of technology. To address these "lacks," we created a simple turnkey solution for any service-based business that automates 90 percent of the work required to *consistently* connect with our customers and ultimately drive revenue. We called it GotFollowup.com.

As we worked on perfecting this solution, we "hoped" that once we demonstrated consistent success with our clients, it would become *a brand standard* and we'd be able to help even more people over time. This is where hope really bit me! I was waiting for my strategic partners to come to the realization that our solution would fill a gaping hole in their business model. I had the age-old "build it and they will come" mentality, which, by the way, is a horrible business strategy. Instead of intentionally scheduling meetings and driving awareness, I simply waited for them to come to me. This ultimately led to a several-year delay in getting the product out, simply because I *hoped* our partners would realize the power of our solution.

One question you might have is, Why did you wait? The short answer is fear of failure. If I'm being honest, I was afraid that if I drove the project, there was a possibility of being rejected and everything would crumble. I finally had the realization that when you only have one option, you have zero options. This is when my mind started playing tricks on me, and I could hear myself saying, "You could lose it all if you push." This is when I had to trust my gut and switch from living in scarcity to living in abundance. Once I made that switch, when I started having intentional conversations about how what I'd built could change the lives of hundreds of business owners, that's when all the pieces started to fall into place.

Have you been in a situation like this, where instead of taking action, you just "hoped"?

So, how did I do it? I created more options. I started scheduling meetings. I placed a value on my time. I looked to the future and visualized my goal. I started chipping away at it every single day, slowly moving closer and closer to what I call *my Oasis*.

[Action trumps hope every day of the week]

"I hope to see you soon."

Entrepreneurs are driven to create something amazing that will make a tremendous impact. Sound like you? Do you work incredibly hard on your business to create financial freedom that will lead to magical moments, then one day realize you've neglected your friends and family because you've been so heads-down. You've become a one-trick pony—all business, all the time, and very little fun (for you and others you spend time with). Then you start asking yourself, Was it worth it? Is being a leader in an endeavor that requires making incredible sacrifices worth it? Take a minute and answer these questions before continuing.

Over the past several years, I've been blessed to develop profound relationships with extraordinary people. We meet at events and always say, "I hope to see you soon!" Surprise, surprise, we rarely get together! This realization really started to weigh heavily on me.

So instead of saying, "I hope to see you soon," I started saying, "Let's rent a giant house and get you and two other families to meet up in April in the Rockies. We'll rent some snowmobiles and wheelers and spend time connecting with each other." Guess what? It actually happened, and it didn't impact my business negatively. In fact, business got better! It did, however, profoundly impact relationships, my friendships, and my family. Being intentional enabled me to connect and create incredible magic moments and sustain lifelong friendships.

[The quality of your life is the quality of your relationships.]

The Exercise, As Promised!

To help you figure out *what* you should be doing intentionally, I've created this exercise that pinpoints exactly where to place your focus. If you do this exercise monthly, you'll completely transform your life.

Step 1. Quantify where you are spending your time. On average, in any given week, how many hours do you spend on . . . ? (Write the number next to the question. You'll need it later.)

1. Career: ____
2. Money: ____
3. Family: ____
4. Personal Growth: ____
5. Romance: ____
6. Friends: ____
7. Fun: ____
8. Health and fitness: ____

Step 2. Understand where you are. In the circular graphic, on a scale of 1–10 (1 being the center of the diagram), rank where you are today in terms of all of these different pie pieces by shading from the center out. If you rank your career as an eight, then shade in the pie piece up to the eight. Once you shade in all the pie pieces, in the box next to each of the categories, write in the number of hours you dedicate to each category. This exercise will 1) give you a clear picture of where you are and what you need to focus on, and 2) give you a clear path to reallocate your time and achieve your desired outcome.

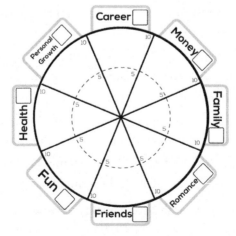

Step 3. Where do you need to refocus your time? You now know where your time is going and where you're starting from. Now, how many hours could you be spending on each of these to achieve the feelings and outcomes you are after?

1. Career: ___
2. Money: ___
3. Family: ___
4. Personal Growth: ___
5. Romance: ___
6. Friends: ___
7. Fun: ___
8. Health and fitness: ___

If you skipped doing the exercise, stop now and go back and do it—you'll thank me later. This exercise can and should be done monthly, because rarely does a single plan of action take you to the Oasis I mentioned earlier. We all have to make slight deviations to our plans, as no journey to the top is a perfectly straight line. We must become adaptable and be open to change to avoid being locked on a path filled with obstacles. We want to get to our Oasis, and Hopium will not get us there.

[Be like water; it can flow, or it can crash. Be like water, my friend.]

Once you go through this exercise, you'll understand that hope will not get you to your desired destination; however, actions and being intentional will.

If you'd like to learn more, scan the QR code to download additional resources or to connect with me directly. I love nothing more than to teach in a simple way that anyone can understand. I love having an impact on people's lives.

[Hope is not a strategy.]

---

[1]Software as a service (SaaS) is a software licensing and delivery model in which software is licensed on a subscription basis and is centrally hosted. SaaS is also known as "on-demand software" and Web-based/Web-hosted software.

Deepak Suthar is an angel investor, speaker, advisor, and entrepreneur in the sales, technology, and business optimization space. He invests in early-stage founders/start-up companies and loves to help them convert their passions into revenue. He wrote this chapter to intentionally create ripple effects that will transcend through the reader and touch the lives of thousands. He loves to speak in front of audiences, large and small. If you'd like to connect with Deepak to learn how he can support you through your journey, you can contact him here:

www.linkedin.com/in/deepaksuthar/
www.facebook.com/deepak.suthar
deepak@gotFollowup.com

CHEREE BURGESS

I Belong!

Was I abandoned, chosen, or both?

I lived this question. I wasn't unlucky, alone, or unloved. I asked because I would look in the mirror and feel unsure how I felt about the girl looking back at me. I was always wondering, "Who is she? Where did she come from? Why does she look like that?" Eventually I got around to asking, "Why did her birth parents not want her? Did they think of her on her birthdays? Did they even love her?" I felt as though this inner voice was always questioning the girl I was on the outside.

Adopted and Knew It

I always knew I was adopted. My adoptive parents were the best parents ever. Not only did they adopt me, but three years earlier they had adopted another baby girl, my adoptive sister. My adoptive mother was not able to have children of her own. Anyone who knew my adoptive parents knew of their love, kindness, and desire to have a family. I still hear the story of the day my adoptive parents and adoptive sister picked me up from the hospital. When the nurse placed me in my adoptive mom's arms, my adoptive sister said, "She is perfect. Let's hurry up and leave before they take her away from us." That is all I know about my birth. The one thing I have never doubted was the unconditional love and support my adoptive parents had for me and my adoptive sister. It was as if we were born to them. For all of us, life and adoption were the most precious gifts God could give.

I was chosen to be with them. They were chosen to be with me. God placed us all together. To this day, my mom still calls us her little angels.

Although I was certain of their unconditional love, I felt restricted by uncertainty. I didn't understand the source of my uncertainty. I did know that it affected me.

Growing Up with a Glitch

I lived with a glitch, a disconnect between my outer appearance and my inner voice.

I was never happy with who I was on the outside. I always wished to be taller, thinner, with different hair, a different appearance.

It was because of all the unknowns. What did my birth parents look like? Did I look like them? What were they like? What were their features, feelings, behaviors?

It's awful wanting to be the other person—whatever that means. I questioned everything. I was terrified of not belonging. I was afraid of failure, never wanting to be the last one picked, always needing to be the favorite. So I became a giver. I didn't need to receive. I felt unworthy and undeserving. Friendships came and went. I did not want to trust people. I set my expectations so high, no one could attain them. I only trusted my family.

I was the biggest Daddy's Girl. I loved sports and was a real tomboy. Wherever my daddy went, I went. I was his little shadow. He was my best friend. As I grew older, that did not change. My daddy was my number one, no matter who was in my life.

Here are the hard parts. I was diagnosed with separation anxiety when I moved away to go to college and then when I moved even farther as I started my career. I could not fix the way I felt on the inside, so I figured I would fix the way I felt on the outside. This led to living with an eating disorder for years. I was always self-sabotaging friendships and relationships, as though I did not deserve to be happy or was afraid of losing someone.

Then came the day I had to face my biggest fear. My dad passed away at the age of sixty-five. A month before he passed, he said to my mom, sister, and me, "If there were one thing I could change, I would have taken better care of myself. Take this as a lesson. Please take care of yourself, if not for me, or yourself, do it for your family."

I questioned, "Why did God take my daddy away?" The only daddy I knew. My hero, my best friend. My biggest fear—of being left—occurred. I went into deep depression. That depression put a crack in my already fragile foundation. It was devastating. But what I learned from it was irreplaceable.

My Son

I knew I had to help others understand deep, wrenching pain. I wanted to help others become healthy and stay healthy. I knew I had to be healthy, strong, and keep living—for my son.

The moment I knew I was pregnant, my first call was to my daddy. I could not believe that in nine months I was going to have a baby. I felt a *shift* taking place in my life. I had a baby inside me who depended on me. My inner voice, my critical, questioning voice, became more and more silent the closer I got to the birth of my baby. Life was altered the moment I held my son in my arms. Holding my baby for the first time, looking at his beautiful face and into his eyes, gave me answers to my questions. It was my awakening moment.

This way my baby. The love of my life. He was my mini-me. Looking at him was a mirror finally reflecting my image, my likeness. I was overcome by unconditional love, overwhelmed with a feeling I had never felt before, along with the realization of the responsibility to protect, to teach, to share the gratitude, the incredible sense of belonging with him. He needed me, and I needed him.

In one moment, my life turned upside down and inside out. I knew. "Yes." I finally knew the answer. It was no longer about unanswered questions. The unanswered questions melted into gratefulness, compassion, complete understanding: *my life is only about doing what is best for my child.* This is how much my birth parents loved me! It was time to accept and resolve my insecurities. I had to overcome my fears and release all that held me back: anxiety, sickness, feeling undeserving and worthless. I did not want to transfer any of these inadequacies to my child. I wanted my child to have the same unconditional love and support I grew up with.

My baby boy has grown to be a loving, strong, and compassionate young man. As his mom, he is my dream come true. I already fear the day I must let him go to follow his own dreams, but I am ready.

I have achieved success in corporate America, raised an amazing son, and found my passion and success in the health, wellness, and fitness industry. Entering the world of fitness enabled me to help others become healthier, as well as giving me an outlet to help others understand the pain of anxiety, depression, and lack of self-worth; but I felt that there was something more out there. Something on a bigger scale. Something that could help everyone. Now more than ever, I had to stop whatever it was that was keeping me from opening myself up for more. I had to keep an open mind and learn to trust.

I was introduced to an amazing company called OsteoStrong. OsteoStrong uses breakthrough technology that can help improve overall health by focusing on the one thing we all have in common: our skeletal system.

As I became more involved and witnessed many people improving their quality of life, reducing or eliminating joint and back pain, managing type 2 diabetes, and much more, I realized this was it. This was "the bigger scale" I was looking for. I knew in my heart that OsteoStrong could have helped my daddy. I took a huge leap of faith and became a business owner. I felt the truth of what my daddy often said: "Taking the first step is the hardest."

I may always feel a bit of uncertainty, a little fear of failure or of not being good enough. I'm human, but a human with purpose. OsteoStrong provided a way for me to continue my daddy's legacy of helping others. My son has given me the strength and courage to be successful. My adoptive parents gave me a family. My birth parents gave me life.

I was not abandoned. My birth parents loved me enough to give me up for adoption. My adoptive parents loved me enough to make me their own.

Every day I get answers to the question, "Who am I?" The answers will keep changing as long as I keep changing. As long as I trust the journey and never forget, I belong! I am part of God's plan.

Cheree Burgess is the owner of OsteoStrong Tuskawilla, offering breakthrough technology that focuses on the one thing we all have in common: our skeletal system. Cheree's lifelong passion in health, wellness, and fitness has allowed her to serve at many levels, including a corporate wellness director, corporate liaison for health and wellness, fitness educator, wellness consultant, and event coordinator for a national fitness education organization. After achieving success in corporate America, the moment she held her son, Kasen, she knew her next career would be a stay-at-home mom. Now that her son is growing up, she has focused her passion into a career with OsteoStrong Tuskawilla. She is carrying on her daddy's legacy of always helping others. She has told many people, "When I walk through the doors at OsteoStrong Tuskawilla, I feel as though I am walking into my daddy's arms."

www.osteostrong.me
www.linkedin.com/in/cheree-burgess-a6ab0b150/

JESSICA GARZA

Own Your Shift

*Sometimes the slightest shift, when done with intention,
can create enormous impact.*

That was definitely the case with my marriage. Like a boulder held in place with a few small rocks and pebbles, all it takes is one shift to set that boulder free. Once rolling, the boulder gains momentum and can change an entire landscape. The path will never look the same just from that one slight shift.

My shifts have largely been within my marriage, yet they have impacted how I experience all of my relationships. If you had told me seven years ago that my relationship would be filled with love, fun, passion, admiration, and adventure, I would have said you're crazy! Seven years ago, my marriage was barely surviving. We were roommates, raising kids, and running our businesses together. Simply put, we were both lifeless and stuck! Constantly experiencing the same things over and over. Having the same arguments, the same sex, the same opposing views . . . it was exhausting and *not* my (or his) idea of a good time. The degree of unhappily-ever-after collided with my fierce commitment to our relationship, leading me on a journey of transformation that started with *me*!

Standing in front of the mirror and blaming the person you see in the reflection is where transformation begins. Take a good look at yourself. What actions/inactions are yours? Your current circumstances, no matter what they are, are a reflection of *you*. Every choice, every belief, every blame all circles back to you. You are the creator of your life. Stop living in victimhood and blaming people for your "unhappily ever after." If you are anything less than joyful, it is no one's fault other than your own. You helped create whatever reality you are living in right now through your actions and inactions. Did you give your power away? Give your voice away? Did you make and keep agreements that didn't align with your desires? Did you do it so you wouldn't be alone, or to protect yourself from being hurt? No matter your reason, *stop* blaming and start getting real with yourself.

If you can't look head-on into the mirror yet, then look at your profile. What are you looking away from over and over in your relationship? What results/experiences are being brought to you by looking the other direction? It all starts with personal accountability. You are responsible for you and *no one* else. Your actions, your attitude, your responses are all your responsibility. Own Your Shit so you can create your own Shift!

What does it take to shift with intention? To shift means to move or cause to move from one place to another, especially over a small distance. Adding intention to this means that you have an aim or a plan. It's really that simple. Knowing what you want (your aim) coupled with small shifts done over time create amazing lasting changes in the long run. When that pebble shifts and the boulder rolls down the hill, the space that opens up takes time to fill in with new pebbles. This is where being in a relationship can be really fun. You and your partner get to decide what you want (intention) and co-create it together (shift) to fill in all of that new open space. Is it more togetherness? Great communication? Better or more sex? What do you want to experience and share together? It's your relationship, so you get to decide together.

The key to this new co-creation is remembering that you are both still *human*! You both have old habits that will creep in from time to time until they don't anymore. Old ways that you used to react to things. You have both been creating this relationship unknowingly one agreement at a time. One disagreement at a time. Moment by moment we create our relationships, whether we do it with eyes wide open in alignment with what we want to experience and share or with our eyes closed on autopilot. When you are consciously co-creating your relationship together, every single time you choose the new co-created way to interact with each other rather than the old habit is a *win*. Each new occurrence is a pebble building that new foundation of your relationship. In my book, *From Fighting To Thriving*, I discuss nine relationship hacks to create the relationship you're seeking, including this one. By catching your partner in the act of doing something awesome, rather than constantly pointing out the things that you wish were different, you are building them up instead of tearing them down. It is a much more enjoyable experience for both you and your partner. Which would you rather experience: someone telling you how awesome you are, or someone constantly pointing out your faults? That's not a hard one to decide. We all like to be appreciated and acknowledged for our efforts. It is part of being human. Show up in your relationship the way you want to be treated, and I guarantee that the momentum of the boulder rolling downhill will be faster than you anticipate!

In the example above, one might say something like, "Well, if I am pointing out all the good my partner is doing, where is my appreciation? When do I get acknowledged?" The first thing I would like to remind you of is that you are responsible for *you*. Remember, you are not a victim of circumstances; you are a creator. What is so cool about this simple shift is that your partner doesn't just get to experience you in a new way, but *you* get to experience you in a whole new way. Less like a victim, and more like an appreciative partner. You will begin to see your partner in a whole new way, and there begins the momentum of the boulder down the hill, carving a new path for your relationship. Any one of the simple shifts I discuss in my book have a similar effect over the long term.

Before this realization and creating my own shift, my life felt like it was on repeat. I was having similar experiences in most of my relationships. I was some kind of victim and everyone else was the reason for my unhappiness. The cycles we live in will continue to bring the same circumstances to us with a different face or a different name, but with the same end result. I see so many people get divorced, often painfully. Marriage in the twenty-first century is here today, gone tomorrow. I can promise you that your cycle of unhappily ever after will undoubtedly follow you into your next relationship until you decide to make a shift. Remember that mirror I mentioned earlier? Yes, it all starts with you. When you are looking for someone else to blame, you've already restarted the cycle.

To shift anything in a relationship is possible. With even the slightest adjustments there can be massive change over time. From wherever you currently are, brand new or twenty years in . . . it does not matter. What matters is your willingness to put in the work and get busy building a relationship worth having.

Where we screw up is when we want it all now. We live in a world of instant gratification, which is so unkind to our partners. We don't see an immediate response to our shift, so we move on to the next. Give each other the patience you would a small child learning to walk. You wouldn't give up on your child . . . ever! So give yourself and your partner some grace as you grow and evolve together. If you have been reactionary in your relationship until now, then creating a relationship with eyes wide open. One new agreement at a time will be brand new for both of you. See this opportunity through the eyes of a child, with excitement instead of drudging through these changes. Work together with love and patience to create the experiences you want to have in your relationship.

Each time a disagreement or response feels familiar, like something you have experienced before, that is your cue to create something new in its place. It really is that simple—notice that I did not say easy. The key is to catch these occurrences day by day and create something new each time. These new agreements build over time and create a whole new experience of what is possible in a marriage.

If you can see yourself in my story and feel your relationships could use an upgrade, then I say go for it! Look to those who have already walked the road you're starting down, whether it's me or one of the multiple of other people obsessed with helping others have great relationships. Find an example of a relationship worth following and follow it! Shift with Intention.

Jessica Garza is a forever-evolving human who lives in Texas with her husband and kids. She has an insatiable hunger for truth and a passion for relationships. She was married twice and once divorced, all to the same man. As a result of these unique experiences, Jess decided to study relationships by interviewing successful partnerships, reading books, attending seminars, and putting what she's learned into practice in her own relationships. Now, having spent the last decade learning through publications and practice what it takes to create a successful relationship, she shares her knowledge and passion with those who may be struggling in the ways she struggled in the past. Her hope is to save others the heartache of learning the hard way. She believes that relationships are the single most important part of the human experience, and she aims to share all she has learned in the most streamlined way possible.

www.nurelationships.com
www.facebook.com/JessGarza13

JASON PRIDE

The Power of Commitment

In life we don't get what we wish, want, or hope for;
we get what we are most committed to.

I believe we are exactly where we are in life based on choices that we have made or the choices we have allowed others to make for us. We are where we are in life because of what we have been most committed to.

My mom died in 2016, just four short years after my dad died. Both died of cancer. However, their deaths had two very different effects on me. When my dad passed I was twenty-one. I chose to cope with it by bottling up my emotions and throwing myself into studies and work. The emotional "avoidance" propelled me to graduate with a 3.9 GPA with a master's degree in accounting and to pass the CPA exam before landing a position with one of the most prestigious accounting firms in the world. Although many people would view this as success, for me this was a form of avoidance that gave me a life of comfort and complacency. It was not yet a life of success and joy.

When my mom died, I chose a different path. After she passed, I reread our old text message conversations. I still have our entire text history saved on my phone almost six years later. Although most of the messages brought happy memories, some did not. There were multiple times where my mom texted, asking me when I was going to visit. My reply was often something like "I'm not sure, probably for Easter. I have to work most weekends right now."

Reading those messages, I realized the job I had been so proud of obtaining was not as alluring as it had once been. It wasn't long before I put in my two weeks' notice. I wanted a life of freedom. A life where I would never have to choose between family and work.

I opened a franchise while focusing on personal development and creating passive income (money earned from an enterprise that has little or no ongoing effort involved). After two years of personal development courses, extensive reading, and a full exploration of the entrepreneurial lifestyle, I was certainly happier than I was before; however, I had not obtained the level of success that I was looking for in business. Or in romance.

Then I attended a Klemmer and Associates seminar and learned a very simple yet life altering concept: *In life we don't get what we wish, want, or hope for; we get what we are most committed to. The only real excuse for not accomplishing something is that we were not committed enough.*

Well, wait a minute! There are plenty of good excuses out there! "Traffic was bad, my boss is an idiot, I didn't get the material from my direct report on time . . ."

Consider this. If I had one day to produce $10,000, could I do it? Most non-decamillionaires, including myself, would likely say no and have a dozen excuses why it wasn't possible. "It takes time to get money, I don't have good credit, I only make $15 an hour." Excuses.

Consider a second scenario: I have one day to produce $10,000 or the two people I love most in life will die. What then? You damn well better believe that I will find a way to create $10,000 in twenty-four hours. So, what changed? The only thing that changed was my level of commitment. The first scenario was just a wish, want, or hope. In the second scenario I am absolutely 100 percent committed and willing to do whatever it takes to achieve it.

Being truly committed to something means it doesn't have conditions. There is never a reason for the commitment to not be upheld. The late Brian Klemmer put it very simply: "It means doing what you say you're going to do." However, I discovered another interesting thing. *I was not always aware of what I was truly committed to.* I felt something shift. *My conscious awareness of what I truly wanted was the missing ingredient.*

It was December 2018. I was about six months into running the franchise and had not been hitting my goal of $20,000 per month. I told myself I was committed to creating $20,000 per month; however, based on results, I apparently wasn't. I say "based on results" because, if you remember, we get in life whatever we are 100 percent committed to. So if we don't have things in life we say we want, then we aren't truly 100 percent committed to them.

What I realized is that although I was (mostly) committed to making $20,000 per month, I was actually more committed to two other things:

1. Being liked
2. Being admired

I cared more about being liked and being admired than I did about creating $20,000 per month. How did this show up? I wanted to be liked, so I wasn't giving direct feedback to employees, and I wasn't enforcing systems and protocols. I was giving away or discounting care to people who "couldn't afford it." I wanted to be admired by having people see how smart I was. I was a CPA and "didn't need help or support" because I knew everything already. (Yeah right . . .)

So, what did I change? First, I started charging the full amount for services and collecting on past-due accounts. I let go of a few staff members. I wrote out systems to be followed and then enforced them. I hired a business coach and leveraged the franchise coaches more. In June 2019 we finally surpassed my $20,000 goal by a staggering $13,000, ending the month at $33,000. We later went on to win new franchise of the year in one of the most competitive markets in the country. But my results didn't just impact my business life.

I had been lonely and unhappy romantically for quite a while, so in December 2018 I made a commitment to find the "girl of my dreams." The first week of February I went on a mission trip to the Dominican Republic (which I almost backed out of at the last minute but decided to do what I said I was going to do and keep my commitment). A couple dozen Dominican doctors volunteered to help our team by translating and providing diagnostic services for us. On our third day there, one of the volunteers, Cristal, caught my eye, and we hit it off right away. I was in love. I even texted my two best friends that day "I am in love" and "I am going to marry this girl." By the end of the day, I (smoothly) got her number. We spent time together and went out every day for the rest of the trip. Before leaving we made a commitment to date long distance, exclusively.

We talked every day and dated long distance for eight months. In October 2019 I asked her to marry me. My brother officiated our wedding at my sister's house ten days later. During my vows I showed her the text message I sent my friends the day we met, saying I was going to marry her. As I write this chapter I can look over and see her sitting on the coach with our three-month-old baby sleeping in her arms. *That* is commitment.

It's simple. Decide what you want, say you're going to do it, and do it. Each of us is capable of creating the life we want by stating clearly what we are committed to and then doing it. Since enacting this principle of commitment, in the past two years I have achieved the following:

1. Met and married my wife. Bought a home together and had our first child.
2. Created passive income that exceeds my living expenses.
3. Achieved two more professional certifications: Certified Valuation Analyst (CVA) and Certified Life Coach.
4. Developed a program that allowed me to triple my monthly take-home income, which I now use when I coach others.
5. Built the franchise, won new franchise of the year, and later sold it.
6. Traveled over twenty times.
7. Began coaching, having helped hundreds of people create the life they deserve, using my business knowledge as a CPA and CVA as well as the personal development concepts I have mastered.
8. Opened a valuation practice where I provide business valuations and consulting services.

I list these things not to gloat but to show what is possible through the power of commitment. One more thing: I now have a job that I love with the company I worked for out of college. Why did I go back? Because I now have a position that is 100 percent remote that allows me to be with my family all day, every day. Plus, I get to do challenging work that I enjoy, with knowledgeable and inspirational superiors.

If you don't have the things in life that you say you want, take another look at your commitment to achieving them. Are you truly committed?

Jason Pride is a CPA, Certified Valuation Analyst, and Certified Life Coach. After earning a master's degree in accounting, he worked for a large accounting firm, then left the corporate world after the death of his parents in his mid-twenties to seek a life of joy and financial freedom. With his knowledge, experience, and self-taught principles, in just three years he built a life that allows him to work where he wants when he wants, built and sold a franchise, invested in multiple real estate deals, opened three other businesses, and worked intensively on personal development. He coaches individuals who want to achieve a higher level of success, and helps hundreds of individuals increase their income and find greater levels of success in business, time management, and relationships. He lives with his wife, Cristal, and son, Aiden, in St. Louis, Missouri.

www.prideinmywealth.com
www.facebook.com/jpride
www.linkedin.com/in/jasonpridehs

MICHAEL GRAHAM

Change or Be Changed

Change: having an effect that is strong enough to change someone's life. A life-changing decision/moment.

I would like to dedicate this chapter to my dear friend
Richard A. Dreyer 11/7/1940–2/5/2022

Rich was my sounding board, spiritual guide, and dear friend that was always there when I needed a push or someone to just chat with. He was part of our family, and was instrumental in my life challenges and shifts throughout my journey.

Are you willing to change things you don't like about yourself, your life? If not, over time, change will happen, and it may not be to your liking. It's up to you to MAKE your change. If not, you will be among millions of people who complain about life but do nothing to change it.

I was an administrator in the nursing home industry, serving the senior population, for about fifteen years. I believed I could make a difference with the residents. I even believed I could change the behavior of the employees so that they would love what they do. I wanted to motivate them in customer service and create an atmosphere of teamwork that would affect their work and even their personal life.

Although I did make a difference with the residents and families, I came to the realization that I could do nothing for the employees. I so much wanted them to enjoy what they did, but I couldn't change their behavior or their attitude. That had to come from them, and it became painful to watch.

The frustration of trying to affect change in others was destroying my health and taking a toll on my body, mind, and spirit. My solution was to numb myself. I knew this was not healthy, so I began working on myself through seminars and self-development courses.

I'm constantly amazed at the people who intersect my life at the exact moment I am in the midst of uncertainty. I met Rich Dreyer, a man who was wise and deeply introspective. I learned a great deal from him, and over time he took on the roles of mentor and friend. I remember the day he walked into my nursing home, *as if he were sent to me.*

We'd had deep conversations before, but this was different. Rich knew many things about me, having discussed personal issues, attended seminars together, and he even helped my wife and me through some relationship issues. He was a master of reading people, their energy, and the energy that a person was giving off.

"What's wrong with this place?" Rich asked. "I noticed the energy was down when I walked in, and you look defeated and worn out."

I sat back in my chair, dejected, knowing all too well what he was saying. His words sliced me open and exposed what I had been thinking for months. I knew I needed to change things, that I was traveling down a dangerous path. I had decided to do nothing because I didn't have an answer. That decision was a recipe for disaster, and, shortly thereafter, I was fired. Let go, transitioned out, terminated. What it's called doesn't matter. I felt defeated, but only briefly.

Was it a coincidence that Rich entered my office to challenge me on my current situation? Or was it God offering me a message of assurance that no matter what was happening in my life, or how uncertain things may seem, that I was OK?

That moment in my life was pivotal. I listened. I heard Rich's words and instead of shutting them out, I shifted my intentions and completely changed my life.

Sometimes we need a push, but the most difficult thing we must overcome is our inability to listen. We have to listen, be open to the feedback. I'd heard many times that I needed to make a change, but, somehow, that day I was open to the feedback from this man, and I didn't discount what I was hearing.

I knew I had to face the dilemma of "What am I going to do next?" I had to rely on my past experiences, all the self-help books I read, classes I took, and people I'd connected with over the past fifteen years.

Rich became my sounding board as I painfully tried to discover who I was. I also benefited from the spiritual guidance of my dear aunt, a Franciscan nun who lived her life around these three questions:

1. What would I do if I had all the freedom in the world to do it?
2. What would I do if I did not concern myself with what people thought of me?
3. What would I do if I did not worry about money?

Supported by good people and sound advice, I embarked upon a new journey. It was time to design the life I'd always wanted. At age forty-five, I knew there would be many challenges. I also knew that if I stayed true to my goals, I would be rewarded along the way.

I started by thinking about the top ten things I wanted to have in my perfect job. I took out a notepad and began outlining exactly what I wanted. Then I allowed those things to manifest themselves in my life. Here is what I wrote down, and I will explain exactly how they showed up in my life:

1. I want to earn six figures, $100,000/year
2. I want to work with seniors or the aging population
3. I want to train or teach something, give presentations in some capacity
4. I want to own my own business at some time
5. I would like the ability to work from home and not have a job that required travel
6. I want to manage people, customers, and be an expert in my field
7. I want to be in the healthcare industry with a company that is successful and have a boss who understands my personality
8. I want to be able to earn more money, maybe a commission or bonus program
9. I want to secure my retirement, put away money for the future
10. I want to work for a company I believe in and that makes a difference in the lives of others

The key to all of this was to write it down. Create it, look at it every day. I even made a vision board and displayed it in my office.

I added another golden nugget: *find a mentor.*

I had just read the book *The Secret,* was beginning to understand the Law of Attraction, and believed that if I thought about something constantly and paid attention, it would show up.

It was a beautiful summer day, temperature in the seventies, when I decided to take a break from agonizing over what the next chapter in my life would look like. Frustrated that nothing was happening, I went outside to sit and ponder.

A new couple had moved in next door, and I watched as the young man walked around, smoking a cigarette, talking on his phone. When he put the phone down, I went over and introduced myself.

The first question I asked was, "What do you do?"

"I work for a health insurance company," he replied. "I am a manager of a sales team."

"Oh really?" I asked. "Are you looking for any salespeople?"

"Yes, I am always looking for good people. Do you have your insurance license?" he asked.

Unsure what that was, I asked, "What does it take to get that?"

As the conversation went on, I continued to ask questions and began checking things off my list.

"Most of our agents work from home," he added, "give presentations, and are experts on advising older adults on insurance needs. We are a Fortune 500 company with great benefits. Most of our agents make six figures, with a great commission structure."

I went back into the house, totally stunned. I found my wife and told her, "You wouldn't believe what just happened. I just attracted my perfect job!"

There were a few obstacles. I knew nothing about insurance, only what I learned from the nursing home industry. I failed my insurance exam the first time, but I was already signed up for training. I had to pass the exam. The first year I made $55,000. My previous job paid $90,000. We adjusted.

By my fourth year, I was earning over $100,000. I realized an eight-year career, amassed a nice retirement package, and moved up the hierarchy as far as I could.

Having created autonomy with my career, there was one big thing on my list that was still missing, the one thing I had always dreamed about: *owning my own business.*

This dream, which had been fixed in my head a long time ago, became my worst enemy. I was very comfortable, made a decent living, had no big issues. Why would I want to change what was working?

As shared by numerous authors, mentors, and speakers, "When God plants a seed of greatness, you better start listening!" I listened. All I heard in my head was, "You can't do that, you'll never make the kind of money you want, you don't have any experience starting your own business." My internal naysayer was loud and clear.

Still, once the seed is planted, things start manifesting, people and opportunities begin to show up, and everything begins to align perfectly for change to happen.

That same neighbor who hired me before was leaving the company to start his own agency. Twelve agents were being downsized from the company, and he was creating an opportunity for them to transition. As fate would have it, he couldn't sustain the income for his family. So, in 2014, I became a partner in this same agency that now has over forty-two agents, five full-time employees, and revenues close to one million.

The business grew in part because of the initial principles I learned and expanded, and the expertise I gained. I have found more mentors, joined mastermind groups, and continued to practice the importance of having *success partners* in all walks of like. I take time for personal retreats and continue to build a network of people who I *choose* to be around.

My newest mastermind leader, Dr. Tom Hill, has taught me to live by another set of principles. Simply put, successful people:

- have a moral obligation to become the very best person possible with our God-given talents.
- have a moral obligation to make a positive difference with every person we meet.
- realize one well-executed idea can change your life forever. One person who is attracted to you because of who you have become can be in your life forever.

I have become a person who strives to be the best and find the good in other people. People are attracted to me because I have become an individual who wants others to succeed, because I know if I help enough people, I will always have what I need.

These and other principles have influenced the way I view myself and my business. I have instilled these principles in my kids, who are now part of the business. Each passing year, as the seasons of life never stop, I remember that the most important thing I have accomplished is what I wanted to do back in that first job: help others change. I just didn't know how then.

The day Rich Dreyer came into my office and gave me real feedback was the day I decided if change is inevitable, I wouldn't let it *happen* to me. I would *manifest my own change*. I have become a person who is willing to change his life.

Paying attention to feedback from others, being open to solutions, and believing with unshakeable confidence that you are not alone is the recipe for CHANGE. Change will happen. That's the one constant we must always recognize. But we can captain our own change. If we pay attention, are aware of signals, surround ourselves with people who have integrity, and accept their feedback, our shift will always be one of growth and self-development.

Michael Graham is the president of Comprehensive Benefits, LLC, a St. Louis–based health insurance agency. The agency was founded in 2014 with ten agents and has since grown to over forty agents in five states, serving approximately twelve thousand clients. His fifteen-year engagement in the long-term care industry and his experience working in nursing homes taught him to respect and appreciate those individuals who have made history and now need help and care later in life. His philosophy has always been, "We take care of those who took care of us." He serves as president of both the Aging Ahead Foundation and Love in Action Community Outreach, a network specialist in the senior market, and co-author of *Senior Care 2.0*. He is finishing his second book, *Flight of an Angel,* the biography of his aunt, a Franciscan nun. Michael has been married to Jennifer Graham for thirty years and has three children.

Michael.graham@mycompben.com
www.linkedin.com/in/mike-graham-10ba5a21/

CRYSTAL TINSLEY

Grip Life with Passion and Purpose

Is someone saying my name?

I lift my head off my steering wheel to discover that I am sitting at a stop sign in the middle of my hometown just as the summer sun is coming up. A friend of mine is pulled up next to me, looking concerned, and through my grogginess and confusion, I felt a sudden jolt of shame and horror rip through my body.

I don't recall what I said to him or what reason I gave for being parked with my head on the steering wheel, but I remember feeling as though he already knew. I was not the same girl I was yesterday. In my sixteen-year-old mind, I was ruined.

The night before, I had invited people to my house while my parents were away repairing their marriage. The past couple of years had been tense. Emotions were out of control in our home, so I had turned to drinking and parties to avoid dealing with what *I couldn't control*. I remember standing in my front yard with a group of friends, complaining that I had a headache. I was ready to call it a night when an older guy said that he had something that would help. He took out a small, black bottle with a gray lid that everyone used to carry 35mm film rolls in and poured out two white pills.

I always thought this guy was handsome, and I trusted him without reason. I had not experienced enough life to understand the situation I was in. After all, he dated one of the most beautiful and popular girls in my hometown. He was in his twenties, so he could not be a bad guy, right?

I remember very little about that night.

The next morning, the confusion about how I ended up alone with him paled in comparison to the overwhelming panic. The guy who I'd thought was so handsome the night before now made my skin crawl, and I needed him away from me, fast. I drove him to his friend's house and sped west, headed home. That is the last thing I remember before I woke up, facing east, with my friend asking if I was OK. How did I get turned around? Why was I sitting there? Everything about that morning is too difficult for me to recall.

I blamed myself. I wanted to blame myself. I bounced around in mental turmoil for months.

My internal dialogue was brutal. "I let this happen. How could I be so stupid? If it was my fault and if I did let this happen, then maybe the awful thing really didn't happen and I am still in control, right? I am ruined now. How could this happen? I'm a bad person now. I'm ruined. I lost what was special about me and nobody will love me now. How could they? What will Dad think? What will others think? What do I have to offer now?" The mental abuse I put myself through was unbearable, so I buried it.

Burying truth will always lead to more pain.

In high school, I became extremely defensive. If anyone provoked me or even made me feel slightly vulnerable—which is what I was most of the time—I would fly off the handle. Sometimes verbally, sometimes physically, and sometimes a combination of the two. I was angry. All the pain that I was hiding was sitting slightly below the surface, waiting to erupt, begging for someone to recognize that I needed to be loved. I used anger and defensiveness to protect myself at a time when I needed love more than any other thing. But I made sure no one knew.

I was suspended from school, did Saturday detentions, started failing my classes. I was drinking. I hated myself. I no longer knew who I was, and I had lost anything resembling passion for living. That was a scary place to be.

Soon, I found myself withdrawing from people even more. Oddly, this is what brought me back to horses and a small amount of healing. Horses were the one thing in life that I had always been passionate about. I lost time when I was with them. I understood them, and I was good with them. When life got hard and I withdrew from everything else that I loved, horses brought me back—more than once.

I'd like to say that this was the pivotal point in my life, and that I rode off into the sunset, but that wasn't the case. I had a lot more to endure before I'd get out of my own way and heal.

I had a tough exterior, which helped me hide my pain and secrets from my family, especially my father. I knew that revealing a truth like I had would set off a time bomb of events that would cause him and a lot of other people more pain. I didn't want anyone else to feel pain that I couldn't contain, so I continued; I disassociated from the real me.

Later, I would meet a man, get married, and then quickly got divorced. I did not know who I was, and I didn't know how to truly let anyone in. The broken young girl inside of me wanted someone to see me and accept me for who I was, to rescue me from myself. Unfortunately, I didn't have the capacity to care for another person's imperfections and mistakes *because I couldn't forgive my own.*

That was the problem! What I finally realized was that when we—especially women—are hurting, we often fantasize about an ideal relationship, the ones we see in movies and hear in song lyrics. The problem with this is that we put the responsibility of our healing onto someone else, and that responsibility is our own. We must let go of victim thinking and be our own hero.

In a few short years, I almost lost my brother and father in separate tragic events, I lost a marriage, the family home where I was raised, my dog, my favorite horse, and was forced to sell the other horses.

I lost me.

Everything I knew was gone. I did not know who I was. This was an even scarier place to be.

I tried to fill a void by dating incompatible people, but it was OK because I never risked showing them who I really was or what I wanted. They never knew me.

I couldn't pay my bills. I was working two to three jobs to keep my head above water, and to avoid time alone with myself. I couldn't buy food and found myself drastically underweight, losing hair, and rarely sleeping. Finally, when I was at rock bottom, I laid in bed and prayed to God, asking him to let me fall asleep and not wake up. I felt rejected by the world and thought that it would be better for everyone if I weren't here. I didn't feel like my life had purpose or meaning.

After that painfully emotional night, I woke up feeling different. I didn't want to experience pain anymore. I didn't have health insurance, so I went to the bookstore and picked up Tony Robbins's book *Awaken the Giant Within*. I was desperate and embarrassed as I scurried to the counter with it under my arm.

That's the day I realized that I was my own problem. I understood no one was coming to rescue me, that I had to be my own hero, acknowledge my feelings, and use them to build a new, stronger foundation for my life.

Since those dark times, I've learned that when our identity is tied to events, things, and places, instead of faith and purpose, we are always at risk of losing ourselves. We are not what has happened to us. That's why having a purpose is so important. Passions, the things we love, remind us of who we are. Passion gives our life purpose. Purpose gives our life meaning. It is imperative that we never let go of the things that are uniquely important to us.

Learning how to change my focus and finally start to take control of my life through fitness and nutrition saved me. I became honest and boldly confronted the truths that had been hurting my heart and soul. I learned the importance of forgiveness. For others and myself.

Since then, I have graduated college, excelled in my career, started a business to help others, placed at a state level fitness competition, and found my way back to horses. I found me. It wasn't easy.

Adversity is a given in life. We will all experience it. That is what builds strength and character. Now, my purpose is to help others discover how they can get a grip on their lives, take hold of their passion, and intentionally live their purpose.

Crystal Tinsley is the owner and creator of GripT Life, a lifestyle brand, created in honor of her father who passed away from pancreatic cancer in 2018. GripT Life promotes mental and physical fitness, helping people to Get a Grip on their best lives. Through speaking engagements, writing, and coaching, Crystal has created a community that helps others move beyond their past and into a future that inspires passion and purpose. When she is not spending time with her horses and French bulldog, she practices what she preaches by serving as an ambassador for 1st Phorm Nutrition, and is an athlete for Precision Fitness and Medical Spa in St. Louis, Missouri. Crystal is currently working on her first book, expected to launch in early 2023. Books saved her life, and she hopes hers will help save others' lives.

She can be contacted at:
www.griptlife.com

DARCY WEBER

The Path of Most Resistance

"Victory will never be found by taking the path of least resistance."
—Winston Churchill

Sometimes I forget how far I've come in such little time. Less than seven years ago, I was a thirty-six-year-old single woman living at Mom and Dad's house in the suburbs of Washington, DC. I had little money in my bank account. I owed thousands of dollars in student loans and credit card debt. My dream was for my father to remodel the carriage house in the backyard so I'd be able to live with some privacy. I didn't have much self-confidence or self-worth and seriously wondered if I was *that* girl whose life peaked in high school.

I was brought up in a wonderful neighborhood and town, surrounded by a loving, supportive family. I was top of my class, scored high on the SATs, lettered in nine varsity sports, and was a state champion in tennis. Pretty. Thin.

I seemed to have it all. Then I tanked.

It turns out the signs were there all along. I started at thirteen with an eating disorder, then chronic depression and anxiety began in my late teens and lasted until my mid-thirties. Suicidal ideations started in my mid-twenties. Those were the worst.

I specifically remember one time when I was on the floor, curled up in a ball, crying uncontrollably. Bottles of prescription medications were laid out in front of me. The emotional pain I felt was unbearable. My brain believed it would have been better for me to die at that point, rather than continue feeling that intolerable sadness all the time.

My biggest fear was that if I failed, I'd be committed to the psych ward and lose my work-related security clearance. The brilliance I knew I was capable of was dimmed because of (what felt like) uncontrollable forces in my brain. The emotional pain was too intense to handle. I believe my brain wanted to self-destruct to save itself from further agony.

Incapacitated with depression and anxiety, I became very familiar with isolation. When my symptoms were at their worst, I'd be bombarded with negative, distorted thoughts. Emotions were indescribably and painfully tortuous. I'd feel miserable, worthless, unmotivated, ashamed, lonely, and hopeless. My ability to function was so compromised that even simple tasks like getting out of bed or showering felt impossible. And when my mind wasn't shut down, the anxiety was so high that even simple decisions were gargantuan tasks. Indecisiveness was paralyzing. I was in survival mode—all my energy was used fighting the war going on inside my mind.

Even though my quality of life was abysmal, I kept going. I had a reason. I kept it to myself. I knew—innately, intuitively, instinctively—what every subconscious force within me told me: *I chose this life, these lessons, my parents before I was born. I knew that the depth of my lows would be counterbalanced by unbelievable highs I had yet to experience. Sharing my battle and eventual victory would help millions of people. I'd be a best-selling author, speak around the world, and become an expert spokesperson on mental health.*

I'm not eloquent. I'm not a good writer or a great speaker. I'm real, but is that good enough? Seriously, I'm petrified. Even writing this short chapter has taken me weeks. As I said, I kept this "reason" to myself because, having been raised Catholic, I knew it would sound crazy. However, this "reason" is why I never acted on my suicidal ideations. It gave me the will to keep going.

Depression: Leading Cause of Sickness and Disability

Virtually everyone on the planet is afflicted or affected by mental illness, whether it be themselves, family, friends, or colleagues. The World Health Organization reports that depression is the leading cause of sickness and disability in the world. That's more than the widely publicized contenders such as cancer, heart disease, and diabetes. Twenty million people try to commit suicide every year. One million people succeed. To put things in perspective, that's roughly the same amount of people who have died from the virus since the pandemic started two years ago.

Despite its widespread acceptance as an illness around the world, depression is one of the most misunderstood illnesses in existence. It causes no outward manifestations like fevers or rashes. It can't be diagnosed with blood tests or x-rays. Depression is invisible, which is why the most common misconception about mental illness is that it's "all in your head." Mental illness is a physical disease that should be treated with the same urgency as any other medical condition.

I could easily have been a sad statistic. Depression could have killed me. It wasn't until I was thirty-six and had tried nine different medicines that I found an incredible psychiatrist. He helped me save myself. I've sent many people to him, knowing he could help them too. I'd like to think I've helped others get their lives back. That's my message: *with the right treatment, mental illness does not have to destroy lives.*

Transcranial Magnetic Stimulation (TMS)

In March 2015, I walked into a Transcranial Magnetic Stimulation (TMS) clinic, had a consult with my seventh psychiatrist, and the rest is history. *TMS is a noninvasive, FDA-approved procedure that uses magnetic fields to stimulate nerve cells in the brain to improve symptoms of depression and anxiety. It has minimal to zero side effects. It's sought by many people who have had an inadequate response to medications.* TMS is like jump-starting a car, but instead it jump-starts brains.

My TMS sessions lasted an hour and a half each. I went five days a week for six weeks. Usually, relief doesn't start until weeks into treatment. Day One brought relief for me, probably because my neurons had been starved for stimulation.

TMS transformed my life. I was able to move out of my parents' house a couple of months after treatment ended. This was the beginning of a new life for which I was *totally unprepared*. My entire life all I wanted to be was happy. I had no idea I'd have trouble acclimating to society. I had more work to do.

Self-Development

At thirty-eight, after almost three years of attempting to reassimilate into society, my real estate coach recommended I attend the Landmark Forum. The Forum helped me deal with the shame I felt having a mental illness. When I first shared my story after moving out of my parents' home, instead of people congratulating me for beating this disease—as they would with someone who beat cancer—they asked me what took so long to get better. Why couldn't I have mustered the emotional strength to change my own thoughts and stop feeling sorry for myself. It made me feel horrible about where I had been.

Eight months later, I was at my first Tony Robbins seminar, and it was more than I could have ever imagined. It was the life school I desperately needed. For the first time, I heard such quotes as, "The amount of uncertainty you can handle is in direct proportion to the quality of your life." "Get in your head, you're dead." "Life is happening for you, not to you." "Proximity is power." If I was destined for a big life, then it was time I take some risks and make changes.

At that Tony Robbins event, I signed up for his Platinum Partners Membership. Platinum Partners could attend any and all of Tony's seminars around the world while also gaining access to a peer group of like-minded, driven, successful people. Joining and completing the year would cost six figures. Who the hell would spend that kind of money on self-development? Well, my intuition to sign up was so strong, I couldn't ignore it. Plus, since TMS, my earnings had increased exponentially, and I had saved enough money to write a check for the entire membership. I figured that if I ran out of money, I could always move back home. It was time to step up and go for broke, which I did, with zero desire to ever look back.

My Platinum year was beyond epic! I traveled to and attended Tony's 13 seminars in Sun Valley, West Palm Beach, San Jose, New York, Chicago, London, Nice, Monte Carlo, New Delhi, Varanasi, Australia, Dubai, Abu Dhabi, Fiji, and Vancouver. I regained self-confidence and self-worth. I finally recognized all the potential and greatness others saw in me. I made friendships that will last a lifetime. It was the scariest yet bravest and best decision I ever made.

The Life I Planned

After my first Tony Robbins event, I read a book called *Your Soul's Plan: Discovering the Real Meaning of the Life You Planned Before You Were Born,* by Robert Schwartz. The author talked about people choosing their life, just as I knew I had. The messages I received from every direction in the universe were that, after feeling lost, alone, and like the only person in the world smothered by depression and paralyzed by anxiety, *I was going to be okay!* Maybe *great!*

It was clear to me that, all along, it was my higher self, my soul, speaking to me and keeping me alive. I again heard the clear message that this life was *my choice.* The pain has a purpose, and my purpose is to help people know what it's like living with depression. It's not sadness or anxiety; they are completely different. When you have depression, you feel worthless, like life is pointless, and you're miserable all the time. You don't get excited about anything because every day feels the same as any other day, so why bother?

If you are like me and have been waiting for someone else's story of hope to help reshape yours, I'm here to be that person. I want my years of suffering from depression to be the catalyst for something great in other people's lives. You don't have to suffer like I did.

Advocates

The hardest part is accepting that each of us needs to be an advocate for ourselves. Be open and communicative with your doctor, with your family and friends. Don't give up if one attempt at feeling better doesn't work. I've now tried sixteen different medications and have been through ninety rounds of TMS. If at first you don't succeed, try again, then try again, then again.

It's not about whether you have resources, it's all about resourcefulness.

I had no one to guide me or to inspire the hope that someone like me, living with depression, could and would live an amazing life. I didn't have anyone to talk to. I felt totally alone. I remember searching "How to acclimate to society after isolating for twenty years" on Google and only finding articles related to people getting out of prison.

That was my epiphany: "Maybe I'm the one who is supposed to be the light for others to help them break free of their personal mental prisons."

I hope that by sharing my twenty-three-year journey to being able to function as a happy, contributing member of society, you can discover a new path. It doesn't need to take that long.

Fast-forward to 2022. For the past year I've been living in one of the world's most beautiful, sought-after destinations in Mexico. I am renting a two-bedroom villa just a few kilometers from the Caribbean Sea, with an outdoor shower, private pool, maid, and gardener. I rescue and rehabilitate injured street dogs and find them forever homes. I have wonderful friends all over the world. As for career, because of my extraordinary work ethic, honesty, innovative thinking, and intelligence, I have aligned myself with some of the most powerful businessmen in the world. It's only a matter of time until I close my first multi-billion dollar international trade deal and become a member of the two comma club (finger's crossed).

To get here, I faced my fears, became comfortable with being uncomfortable, and delved into the unknown. I'm self-employed, work my own hours, and choose with whom I work. I am proud to be working with some of the highest achievers and most successful companies in the world.

It's about opening up to discover what is possible by following your intuition and surrendering to what life brings your way. If you are someone who lives with depression or any other mental illness, please know that there are places where you can go that will help you help yourself. It would be my privilege and honor to be among the first you seek out to do so.

If you are depressed, have an eating disorder, or have had thoughts of suicide, please seek help:

- National Suicide Hotline: 1-800-273-8255; suicidepreventionlifeline.org/
- National Alliance on Mental Illness: www.nami.org/Home Depression and Bipolar Support Alliance: www.dbsalliance.org/ American Psychiatric Association: www.psychiatry.org/
- National Eating Disorders Association: 1-800-931-2237; www.nationaleatingdisorders.org

Darcy Weber battled depression and anxiety for more than twenty years, overcoming isolation, self-defeating thoughts, suicidal ideations, and eating disorders to become the woman she is today. Successful, shockingly intelligent, funny, and humble, you feel like you've known her forever. Her bravery and empathy are extraordinary. She never backs down, will always help someone in need, and can achieve anything if she puts her mind to it.

Given the overwhelming prejudice around brain health conditions (aka mental illness), especially the stigma against getting any pharmacological treatment, Darcy was advised to use a pen name for this chapter. But Darcy wants to live in a world where one doesn't have to be "brave" to be real. So in true Darcy style, she chose the vulnerable route of openly sharing her story of recovery in hopes of helping others.

Raised in a DC suburb, Darcy graduated from the University of North Carolina at Chapel Hill and has worked in government contracting, financial services, management consulting, real estate, and medical supplies. Currently living in Mexico, she devotes her free time to rescuing injured street dogs, playing tennis, and traveling.

Please connect with Darcy through the following link. She would love to hear from you.

linktr.ee/dmw6

Mindcraft: The Game of Belief

Today is going to be an amazing day.

It was Wednesday morning at 6:45 a.m. Before I got out of bed, I said to myself, out loud with certainty, "Today is going to be an amazing day. I don't know what will happen, but I know it is going to be amazing." At 9:07 a.m. I got a text from a friend asking me to be a part of her book project.

This is my story about my journey into shifting with intention and manifesting my best life. I started becoming a conscious creator about three years ago. I didn't really know what I was doing. I just decided to start asking the universe for what I wanted. Honestly, the very first time I asked the universe for something I desired, it manifested almost immediately. I kept it very simple and, looking back now, I know that was key. I presented the universe with my desire and went about my business. I didn't think about how it would happen or when it would happen; I just had faith it would; and it did.

For forty years of my life, I had no idea how powerful my thoughts were. I let fear, anxiety, and insecurities drive my thinking and, in turn, drive my life. My self-concept was poor, and I tolerated toxic, abusive relationships. I am a survivor of domestic violence. I endured years of physical, emotional, financial, and verbal abuse. I was controlled and estranged from my family and friends, a result of him wanting to keep me dependent. Unfortunately for him, he chose the wrong girl.

Getting back on my feet was not easy. My efforts to be independent were sabotaged. Being a single mom with three young kids made it difficult to finish school. There were times I wanted to quit, but I persisted.

I hadn't considered myself a survivor of domestic violence until I was trying to explain to my kids' schoolteacher that I was uncomfortable attending a meeting with my abuser. In that moment, I was conscious of the language I was using.

"So, they are asking you to sit in a room with your abuser?"

I replied, "I've never considered myself a survivor of domestic violence, but I guess I am." Notice I keep using the word *survivor* and not *victim*. I debated whether to even include my abuse history in this chapter, because it is not a part of my history that I give any energy to. It is, however, part of my journey, and my hope is that my story will be an inspiration to at least one person.

There are many reasons people get stuck in victim stance. It can become a mindset, a comfort zone, a way to draw attention, a way to cope, or a way to diffuse responsibility for current circumstances. I am fortunate to have a survivor mindset. I'm not the type to replay past events. I'm more of an out-of-sight, out-of-mind type. It's not that I've never looked back at my past, but I don't let my past circumstances define my present or my future.

I used to always joke that I must have been really bad in a past life to keep experiencing toxic relationships, and yes, I've had more than one toxic relationship/marriage. Now I realize my previously negative mindset attracted those toxic men into my life. It was the same relationship but a different name, a different face. I wanted a healthy, loving relationship, but my mindset and subconscious belief was that I only deserved toxic men. I thought it and spoke it into existence.

After my third marriage failed, I finally decided I deserve to be loved, adored, cherished, honored, protected, and respected. I decided this because my third husband did not provide these things. Being loved ... and respected were noticeable by their absence.

About three years ago I asked the universe to send me a man who would love and adore me. I kid you not, almost immediately I got a text from someone I had dated a year prior.

He said, "I don't know why, but you just popped into my head."

Of course, I knew why. He was someone who had loved and adored me, and I had sabotaged the relationship because even though I wanted to be loved and adored, I didn't know how to accept it or give it. Today I love deeply, and for the first time in my life I'm allowing myself to be vulnerable.

But before I could start accepting my desires, gifts, and blessings, I had to work on my core beliefs and self-concept. I started talking kinder to myself and saying self-concept affirmations every day, numerous times a day. I had to reprogram my subconscious mind. At one point, I had way overcomplicated my efforts to be a conscious creator. I was saying affirmations either verbally or in my mind most of my waking hours, watching videos of manifestation coaches constantly, listening to subliminal recordings during the day and while I slept. It started to feel like a full-time job. I was anxious and frustrated. I wasn't getting what I wanted when I wanted because I was operating out of a place of fear and lack. I will say that the self-concept affirmations I said every day did help shift my subconscious. However, creating my best life shouldn't have felt like work, and I shouldn't have felt anxious and frustrated.

I stopped listening to subliminal recordings and watching manifestation coaching videos. I stopped saying affirmations all day every day. I remembered back three years ago when I'd manifested effortlessly. I went back to keeping it simple. Today I start every day by thanking the universe, my spirit guides, God, and other higher powers for my gifts and blessings. I remind myself I am worthy of all good things and everything I desire. I operate on faith, confidence, and belief. My desires for what I want out of life have been consistently the same.

I have been through some tough times, but through it all I was blessed with an abundance of support from family and friends.

I have picked up and started over three times.

- After one marriage, I had to recover from bankruptcy because he was a financial disaster.
- In 2018, I was diagnosed with stage 0 cervical cancer—the stage right before it turns to cancer. I was terrified, but I was determined to be OK. I had to go out of town for my daughter's soccer tournament that same day, and one of my best friends insisted on going with me so I wouldn't be alone.
- I had two surgeries, one consisting of a partial hysterectomy. I recovered completely and am grateful to be healthy today.

Everyone has always said to me, "You are the strongest person I know." I wore that like a badge of honor for a long time. Guess what? Being strong all the time is exhausting. Why should I have to be strong?

I decided I didn't want to be known as strong. I thought I wanted to be known as lucky, but it is not about luck. I call it *Mindcraft—a combination of mindset and determination.* Mindcraft is believing I am worthy of experiencing love, joy, happiness, peace, and financial freedom. The day I drive my dream car off the lot, I will be one happy girl. For years, fear and doubt kept me from taking chances or allowing myself to be vulnerable. I sat back and watched other people get the things I wanted. I admired these people for being brave enough to go after what they wanted. Why shouldn't I go after what I want? Fear and doubt! What a twosome.

The more I let go of fear and doubt, the more gifts I started to receive. In a three-month span, I was approached with a new job opportunity with a significant pay increase, an opportunity to start a new business, and this writing opportunity. My friends and family know I am a conscious creator—the term they use is "manifester." They poke fun at me for *manifesting.*

What they don't understand is that they manifest as well, but they manifest on autopilot. All I have done differently is become mindful of my thoughts. It took some trials, tribulations, and tears (shh, don't tell anyone I cried; I'm strong, remember?). Today I notice fewer negative thoughts sliding in. I wake up grateful every day. I am human. Life still happens. But my attitude makes a difference in the outcome. My happiness is the product of my attitude and mindset.

My motto: "Think and speak your best life into existence." If you let it, life is an experience with unexpected gifts. When you have a positive mindset, you can reveal strengths you didn't know you even had. Sorrow can turn to joy. Dreams will blossom. Never give up, because when life is the hardest, shift happens.

Jill Kneemiller, MA, LPC has been a Licensed Professional Counselor in Missouri since 2013. She holds a bachelor's degree in psychology and a master's degree in professional counseling. She went to Lindenwood University on dance, academic, and leadership scholarships. By day she works full time as a Utilization Review Behavioral Care Advocate for an insurance company. She is also the co-owner of Greenlite Wellness Center where she facilitates group and individual therapy. She specializes in substance abuse therapy with over ten years' experience in the field.

Jill is the mother of three strong-willed, independent, beautiful young women. She enjoys her life to the fullest and finds time to laugh every day. She is passionate about self-care and nutrition and never passes up an opportunity to see a beautiful sunset or sunrise.

Jill can be reached at:

GreenliteWC@yahoo.com
www.Facebook.com/Jill.Kneemiller/
www.facebook.com/Greenlite-Wellness-Center-103988928867832
www.instagram.com/jill.e.k/
www.linkedin.com/in/jill-kneemiller-ma-lpc-29a62a46

RYAN O'DONNELL

You're Not Done. You're Going Back.

"Sir, do not move. You've been involved in a serious accident."

These were the words I heard while I was on the cold, wet pavement at 11:58 p.m., February 26, 2021. It was Friday night, no different than any other in St. Louis, Missouri. I had the pleasure of hanging out with friends who I don't get to see very often. I own a property investment company that keeps me busy most days of the week. I was with Ruth, a friend I had met a few years prior, and Christian, whom I've known for most of my life. We started the night at a local pizza restaurant. We were having a great time, so we decided to leave and go to a new place to finish off the night. We had no idea our lives would never be the same.

I walked to my parked car, opened the door, and set my box of leftovers on the passenger seat. The three us of looked both ways and started crossing the street. I followed closely behind Ruth and Christian, then glanced at my phone for only a moment.

The next events were a blur, but video footage caught by a nearby gas station helped fill in the blanks. A 2003 Hyundai Elantra sped through the traffic light. The brakes were tapped for a quick second as the driver noticed us crossing the street, before deciding to continue and hit us at a whopping 50 mph, twenty miles above the speed limit. Ruth was the first one hit; she flew into the air. I was directly behind her. The impact caused me to roll onto the car. We both landed on the sidewalk. Christian was holding Ruth's hand when it all happened. He did not get hit by the car, but it was a near miss. You would think he was fortunate, but for him, having to live the rest of his life with those images is painful.

I did not see the car before it hit us. None of us did. Christian said he thought he saw headlights. I remember it like this: a smack (as if falling from a ten-story building onto the pavement), then nothing, blackness. While I was unconscious, I saw a colorful electrical current. It carried me to a white space. It felt quiet and peaceful.

As I'm realizing I've died, I heard a loud voice, booming like thunder.

"You're Not Done! You're Going Back!" The words were crystal clear, and I knew God was talking to me. Immediately after the word "back" I was back in my body, which felt like it had been hurtling through the galaxies.

Next thing I knew, I was waking up in a hospital room. I felt the pain. I opened my eyes when a detective asked me if I remembered anything from the accident. I did not. I closed my eyes, then opened them again and saw my mother, who told me Ruth had also been hit and did not make it. That was the last thing I wanted to hear.

Why didn't she survive? Why did I?

The doctors told me I had several broken bones, including my fibula, my tibia, my right wrist, five ribs, three vertebrae, and a compressed disc. They told me I may never walk again. I was lucky to be alive. The doctors said it was a miracle, and, if anything, I should be brain dead or at least a quadriplegic.

The detective came back and told me that the St. Louis City Police were trying to locate the driver who hit my friend and me while we crossed the street. Right after we were hit, the police started a pursuit, but it ended after the driver went into oncoming traffic on the interstate. However, they did find the vehicle parked in front of an ex-police officer's home because the doorbell camera caught the driver when she ditched the car. They traced the vehicle to the driver and reported she had been gambling and drinking at the casino before the accident, as well as possibly engaging in a methamphetamine delivery.

I continued to defy the odds over the next year, which was difficult because of the healing process. I spent two full weeks in the hospital before I decided I wanted to go home and sleep in my own bed. I was picked up from the hospital and placed across the back seat of the car. The best thing about arriving at my home was being greeted by Angel, my doting house cat of eighteen years.

I was bedridden for five weeks. Eventually, I was able to get out of bed on my own. Angel took care of me, walking with me everywhere, making sure I was OK. Almost a year later, I returned the favor when he became sick and passed away in my arms.

I had never been very spiritual or religious before this accident, other than the traditional upbringing I had. Since that experience, I do believe there is some type of higher power that greets us when we pass. I was told that "You're not done. You're going back."

I have more to do, but what could that be? I thought about this a lot during my recovery. I feel as if my purpose here in life is to help others. That's my goal, starting with a request to God every morning to send me someone who needs some sort of help. He sends them. Random strangers, my work colleagues, people who just need a little help. I am still on my journey of figuring out what exactly He meant.

As I write this, it will be a year next week since my accident. A lot happened during my recovery. The woman who was driving the car that hit us had a history of driving while intoxicated, drug and drug paraphernalia possession, and unlawful use of a weapon. She has since been charged with leaving the scene of a crash resulting in death and resisting arrest, and she is currently awaiting trial. Hopefully, she will have a long time to sit and think about the decisions she's made in life, one of which unfortunately cost Ruth her life.

I owe a lot to the ones around me who helped during my time of recovery. My mother came over every day to help me while I was on bedrest. She helped take care of Angel when I couldn't feed and water him. Yes, she also made sure I was fed and watered. At the office, my assistant Nicole went above and beyond for me, taking care of everything. I could not have accomplished much work, if any, without her. I am thankful for my loved ones and cherish them dearly.

Today, I'm back at my usual daily routine. I have a successful property investment company, Turn Key Property Providers, located in Cahokia Heights, Illinois. We buy rental properties, flip them, and resell them. I haven't allowed the accident to slow me down more than necessary, especially since the business is growing rapidly with more properties and employees. I feel blessed to have a second chance. God truly blessed me after the accident. No doubt about it!

Ruth is living vicariously through her loved ones. I will not let her die in vain. Every day, I understand that life is precious and there is no promise of tomorrow. You can be having a great time with your friends, one moment eating pizza, then gone the next.

Just because I was hit by a car and couldn't walk for months, I'm no quitter. As soon as I was able, I pulled myself up and put myself in my car and drove to work, my desk chair serving as a pseudo wheelchair. On top of that, I spent three days a week in therapy and three days a week at the chiropractor.

God is good! I'm stronger than I was before the accident, mentally and emotionally. I wake up every day with a new outlook on life. I will continue to thrive and grow. It's been a long year, but now I am 90 percent back to normal. I did get a second chance at life, because God decided it just wasn't my time. I have a lot more that I need to accomplish before I go home, and I plan to do it. Now, every morning, I wake up and tell God that I'm grateful for everything that He's given to me in this life. I also ask Him to place anyone or anything in front of me where I can find a way to help. I no longer take life for granted.

Ryan J. O'Donnell owns Turn Key Property Providers in Cahokia Heights, Illinois, and buys, flips, and sells investment properties to clients all around the world. Ryan mainly deals in single family and large packages of homes. He was born in 1975, at Memorial Hospital in Belleville, Illinois, and grew up in the Belleville suburbs, about fifteen miles east of St. Louis, Missouri. He was raised by his mother, Joyce, who was the caretaker at home, and his father, Frank, who was a Real Estate Investor until he passed away in 1990 when Ryan was fifteen. He has an older brother, Mark, who is also a co-owner in Turn Key Property Providers. Ryan still lives in Belleville on a golf course, and he shares his home with his two cats, Charlie and Sampson. He enjoys traveling and is always down to help anyone in need to the best of his ability.

www.stlpropertydirect.com

RICH GROGAN

From Self-Bullying to Success

I sprang up from bed, yelling "DON'T TOUCH ME!"

I was sweating, with fists clenched, a racing heart, and enough adrenaline pumping through my veins that I could've punched a hole through the wall.

I looked around the room, but nothing was there, just the images in my head. It was 2:00 a.m. and I was completely safe in my own bed, but the nightmare was real. I was twelve years old again and one of the meanest bullies on the team had trapped me in the locker room and I had no idea what to do to protect myself. I was frozen with fear, just like every other time I'd been bullied.

Often when we hear the word "bullying" we only think of examples like mine in the locker room, kids being bullied on the playground, or on social media. The truth is, this locker room bullying causes self-bullying, which is just as destructive.

We may have been bullied when we were kids, or it could have happened last week on social media. Bullying hurts, and it leaves emotional scars. Having personally experienced it, I know how deep those scars cut.

My point is, when we continue to focus on those painful memories and allow those negative thoughts to control the way we think about ourselves, we can never fully live our best lives. We often put more trust into the thoughts, words, and opinions of others, who don't really know us, than we do in what we know to be true about ourselves.

It's like allowing a weed to grow in your beautiful garden. The weed is the negative thought and limiting belief. The garden is your beautiful mind.

What do weeds do?

They grow deep roots and suffocate anything around them, the same thing negative thoughts do to a positive mind.

I believe the meanest, nastiest bully we will ever face is the bully we hear in our minds, caused by thoughts of worthlessness and self-doubt.

Two of the ways I bullied myself were my unhealthy obsession of comparing myself to others, and the need to prove that the people who doubted me were wrong.

It became my personal mission to give a big "F U" to the world and anyone who ever told me I wasn't good enough, smart enough, or tall enough.

Sure, this drove me to do things that people said I couldn't do, but I ended up spending all my time fighting meaningless battles against the ghosts in my head.

I've always had an excellent work ethic and the belief that I could outwork everyone. It's one of the virtues of growing up on the farm. Still, deep down, I believed I would never be more than a "poor, dumb farm boy." I still hear this in my mind, even today. It is amazing how deep those roots are embedded.

Along with working hard, I always had more than enough energy.

Now, I've never been officially diagnosed with ADHD, but it's apparent to anyone who knows me that I've got some form of it. I used to think this was a curse, especially as a kid, but now I choose to use it as strength. That said, I've learned that any strength can quickly become a weakness if uncontrolled.

That's exactly what happened.

On the outside, I had my life together. I was a PE teacher, had a beautiful family and my own business. I'd opened a martial arts academy, filmed four fitness videos, and had achieved my 4th Degree Black Belt and Master instructor certification in Korea. But on the inside, my foundation was cracked and crumbling. I suffered through six grueling knee surgeries and a serious health scare. Financially, I went through two bankruptcies, multiple car repossessions, and I almost lost my home to foreclosure. The price of feeding my fragile ego, and making it appear all was great, nearly cost me everything. I was self-bullying, and it had to change.

My shift started in 2008. I was in my office, crying and wallowing in self-pity, along with countless other victim-minded thoughts. I wondered if I should give up on my business, and questioned why God wouldn't let me win. Then the strangest thing happened; I swore I heard God say to me, "So, what are you going to do, big boy? You talk about perseverance and not giving up, but here you are thinking about giving up. This is your chance. Are you just going to lie there and cry, or are you going dig deep and utilize the gifts I've given you to make a difference in the lives of others?"

In my selective hearing, I missed the last part, "in the lives of others," and it took a few more years to take that in.

In 2012, I started listening to a man named Zig Ziglar, and my life was changed forever. Against the wishes of my friends and family, I took another huge leap and quit my teaching job to focus full time on my martial arts business.

I started buying Ziglar's books and recordings and listening to them anytime I was in the car. "Automobile University" he called it. I remember picking my kids up from school and them asking me, "Dad, do we have to listen to Zig again?" Now they can quote him as well as I can.

I started attending conferences and encountered countless other authors and successful people I wouldn't otherwise know existed. I found that every one of them had some things in common. They were all extremely successful, genuinely happy, and were an encyclopedia of knowledge from the books they'd read.

Prior to 2012, I barely knew I could read, because I chose not to. Now I have over three hundred books on my bookshelf and five hundred books in my Audible account, with over twelve hundred listening hours and forty journals full of notes.

I went from a scarcity to an abundance mindset and found that, for me, the best way to defeat the bully within was to self-educate.

On December 17, 2017, I got baptized. I finally found what I had been missing. I'd known about the Bible. I went to church as a kid. But regardless of how often my Grandma Bonnie would ask me if I was putting God first, I never was.

My shift finally happened when I realized my purpose: **to empower others with hope and confidence to believe in themselves.** I focused on putting God first, spending more time with my family, and helping others instead of trying to prove they were wrong.

I started using Zig Ziglar's approach: *You can have everything in life you want, if you will just help enough other people get what they want.*

I am now a published author, certified Zig Ziglar speaker, trainer and coach, and successful business owner.

I've had difficulties, and I still have battles with the bully within, especially on days when I allow my mind to focus on the wrong things. But now I am building on a solid foundation.

Based on my life experiences, I've developed a process that has helped me and countless others: **The ABC's to Become Bully Proof,** which teaches you how believe in yourself and stand up to any bully, both real and in your mind.

Bully Proofing is a way of life; it takes continuous focus and practice to remain confident. Here are the three key points of the program:

• "A" is Awareness and Avoidance, being aware of everything going on around you and everything you allow into your mind and body. A harmful way that I bullied myself was allowing destructive thoughts to control my mind, instead of using my talents to help others.

• "B" is Believing in yourself, putting on your Bully Proof Armor. Your Bully Proof Armor is strengthened through self-respect. There are things you can do to better yourself, like doing your best at everything you do, reading, self-educating, surrounding yourself with positive influences, daily affirmations, and positive self-talk. Your Bully Proof Armor protects your most vulnerable areas, your heart and mind. These are also the two areas that all bullies attack.

• "C" is Communicate Clearly with your Confident posture (head up, shoulders back, eyes forward). The way you carry yourself will emotionally affect the way you feel about yourself and the way others see you. You either carry yourself believing you're a victim or a hero.

Following these three simple steps and practicing them daily helped me shift from self-bullying to success. The ABC's will help protect you from any bully you face, both real and in your mind, so you can live your best Kickin'Life, getting back up each and every time life knocks you down and living your life to its fullest.

I'll conclude with my favorite Zig Ziglar quote:

You are what you are and where you are because of what has gone into your mind. You can change what you are and where you are by changing what goes into your mind.

Master Rich Grogan is a Master Martial Artist, 6th Degree Black Belt, and a Bully Proof & Self-Defense Expert with over forty years of experience.

He's an author, inspirational speaker, Ziglar Life Coach, host of the "Grogan's Bully Proof & Kickin'Life" Podcast, and owner of one of the largest martial arts academies in the Midwest.

His life's work and passion is empowering millions of people with hope and self-confidence, utilizing his unique uplifting messages to audiences of all ages on leadership, life skills, character development, and becoming bully proof. For more information about Master Rich Grogan, or to buy his books, journals, bully proof program, and apparel, or to hire him to speak at your next event, visit his websites:

www.grogansbullyproof.com
www.youtube.com/grogansbullyproof
www.facebook.com/grogansbullyproof
www.instagram.com/grogansbullyproof/
www.linkedin.com/inmastergrogan/
www.bullyproofpodcast.com/
www.grogansmartialarts.com

Breaking Generational Curses and Becoming Yourself

Tony, someday Kailee is going to choose a guy like you and marry him. If she were to choose today, would you be happy with that choice?"

That was the question I heard as I sat there defeated, having lost, yet again, my battle with anger and exploding on my daughter. At the time, I was not sure if the voice was God, my guides, or my higher self, but it was a distinct voice. The question definitely caught my attention.

My reply was, "Hell no! I'd kill him!"

Then the voice responded back in a gentle and loving tone, "Well, she is watching you. You have work to do!"

I fell to my knees in tears, letting the sound of those words resonate and sink deeply into my mind. Picking myself up off the ground, I asked aloud, "How do I fix it? How do I get past the anger? I've tried everything and failed miserably!"

This is where I answer the question you are probably asking. "Yes, I hear voices. Guess what? I talk back to the voices too! Ha, ha!" But I'm not crazy. Well, maybe I'm not.

I tried therapy. I went to church, I tried to hand it over to God, asked God to give me strength to overcome. I tried to just think positive. You name it, I tried it to overcome the "demons" of anger.

Every day I would wake up to an inner battle. "Tony, don't get angry today. You can do this! Kailee needs you to be a happy dad." I was scared. I felt out of control of myself.

My daughter never knew which side of me she was going to get. One minute I'd be having fun, joking around, playing, and it was great. The next minute I was screaming, yelling, being abusive—at times physically, mentally, and emotionally—and throwing things across the room.

I would even get mad when she started crying! Why? Because I hurt her and made her cry! I would project my anger at myself onto her. I hated that I, the man who is supposed to love and protect her physically and energetically, was causing her pain. I would either leave the room, yell at her to stop crying, or tell her to go to her room. Then I would calm down, apologize, tell her I'm working on it, and that it will get better. The cycle continued.

At that time, I was a Christian, so I went to two separate pastors, both of whom told me that while I may be riddled with anger my whole life, I should keep seeking strength in God. God would give me strength. They pointed to scripture that affirmed their advice, which later I came to believe was a misinterpretation of what Jesus was actually teaching. I felt defeated. I had tried everything up to that point, and if God wasn't going to help me overcome, then "maybe I am going to be angry my entire life," I thought to myself. I mean, that was all I'd ever known my whole damn life. My dad, my brother, my mom, they all suffered from the wrath of anger. I felt at the mercy of God and life.

Sitting with the scripture, as well as the advice from the pastors, I got angry. Shocker, right? I yelled at myself, of course. "Why does God want me to suffer? Why does he want my daughter to suffer?" That just didn't make sense.

It was my anger at the senselessness of it that made me dig deeper. I vowed that night that I would overcome anger or die trying. I was tired of being miserable. I was tired of being unhappy. I was tired of being so volatile. I was tired of not being the dad I wanted to be for my daughter. I wanted to be the man who I knew deep down I could be. I began a journey that created an amazing shift in my life, and in my daughter's life.

The Backstory

Before I explain what I did to create the shift, you'll need a bit of the backstory. Not all the backstory, because that would be a long-ass book in and of itself. I am going to summarize the key events that led me to hear that voice and decide to explore healing and awakening. Then, I will get into the shift and share conversations I had with my dad before he passed in 2020.

The first event was when my wife, my daughter's mom, died accidentally from an overdose. I found her on the couch where she'd passed in her sleep. That event led me to be the sole caretaker of our daughter, who was five at the time. It has been eleven years since my wife passed.

Little did I know the power of her death and the Divine orchestration that would lead me to where I am today. I will share this awareness at the end. Yep, I'm making you wait until the end!

The second event was going through a divorce after my wife died. I got remarried two years after she died. It did not last long, and both of us were extremely unhealthy. This, by the way, was my fourth marriage—the one that woke me up.

Recognizing that I was the common denominator in all my relationships, I realized that if change was going to happen, it had to be with me. That was when I heard the voice in my head telling me I had work to do.

The Shift

"You know this is going to happen to you," my brother said to me in the elevator as we were leaving the hospital. We'd been visiting my dad after an emergency triple bypass surgery.

"What's going to happen to me?" I asked.

He replied, "You are going to have a heart attack, too." My brother was never one to sugarcoat things.

I said, "No I'm not!"

He fired back, "Yes, you will. It runs in the family." He'd had a heart attack at forty-one, and has had a couple more since then, which was why he was saying this to me.

I fired back, "Do you know why it runs in the family? Because we're a bunch of angry assholes, passing on the same bullshit stories! This is not happening to me! I am breaking the generational cycles and changing our family tree!"

My dad's surgery happened around the same time I'd heard the voice and was beginning my journey. I was going to beat anger, even though I had no idea how, and could not imagine the journey I was about begin.

Fast-forward three years to 2017. I heard this voice whisper in my head (you catching the theme here?) "Set him free."

Confused, I responded aloud, "Set him free? Who and what are you talking about?"

The voice whispers back, "Set your dad free."

I asked, "Set him free from what?"

"Tell him thank you for the way he raised you."

I pushed back. "Oh, hell no. My dad and I don't have a relationship like that. No way can we be that vulnerable with each other."

The voice was relentless.

I exclaimed, "Fine! But it won't end well!"

I went to my dad's and started the conversation with him. "Dad, thank you."

He responded, "For what?"

I said, "Thank you for the way you raised me."

He got defensive and exclaimed, "I showed you love when you were younger!"

I calmly said, "Dad, I am not attacking you, and there is no need to be defensive. Thank you for the way you raised me. Because of you, I know now what not to do."

Then the voice told me, "Ask him if he was shown love when he was a kid."

I thought to myself "Are you kidding me?" But I knew if I resisted it would get very uncomfortable for me, so I asked, "Were you shown love when you were a kid?"

To my surprise, my dad responded, "No."

I then asked, "Was your dad shown love? His dad? And his dad?"

Every answer was a "No!"

I said, "Dad, I'm changing that. I am healing and want you to know that I'm good, and we're good. Thank you! I love you!"

May 2020, I had a dream about my dad's death. I asked for further understanding and learned that he was going to be dying soon. It overwhelmed me. I'd never experienced anything like that before.

I'd been on a major spiritual awakening and healing journey for about a year, committed to shattering generational curses. Since I'd asked him the questions, there was a difference in my relationship with my dad. It was more peaceful and loving. When I had the dream about his death, I was instructed to talk with him because he was holding on to make sure we were OK. He'd created his own suffering for several years after my mom died, holding on to guilt and shame for the way he treated all of us. My channeling revealed this to me. My dad was suffering from diabetic dementia at this time, and I wasn't sure if he would be able to have a coherent conversation or remember any of it. I was assured that he would. My conversation with my dad confirmed the prophetic information I was given. My dad was more open sharing with me, although still reserved, because, energetically, he knew I knew what he was experiencing. I assured him that we were OK, and that it was safe for him to let go when he was ready. Two months later, he exited his earthly hell and transitioned over to freedom and peace.

Aggressively pursuing my inner work has allowed me to break generational traumas and patterns. It allowed my relationship with my dad to shift. Although he was still angry, he was more at ease. I was able to show my dad a new way before he exited here. Now, he is one of my guides, and he visits regularly.

Becoming Myself

Going on my inner healing journey hasn't just affected my life. It changed my relationship with my daughter. It healed generations of trauma and has opened the path for future generations.

This is my purpose. This is why I've experienced everything I have, so that I can teach others how to do the same. How to become themselves, either again or maybe for the first time. How to manifest a life that's not only exciting and fun, but the life of their dreams. To *laugh through life.*

Breaking generational curses isn't just for me, or for certain people. It is for *anyone* courageous enough to face themselves and say, "This cycle ends with me!"

If you recall, I alluded to the Divine timing of my wife's death. Now, I'll share it with you. Through my healing journey I intuitively came to know the magic of my wife's death. Although painful at the time, it was orchestrated beautifully. My wife died to save me. Her death saved me. She gave me a daughter, then died, to save me. I had to have a daughter, and my wife's death to create the shift! It's a beautiful love story!

Now, I can confidently say I am the man I've always wanted to be. I am the dad I have always wanted to be. I continue to evolve and grow into the next highest version of myself, stepping deeper into my power. I have amazing, spiritual, "weird," gifts that allow me to help people shift their lives and create their dreams, learning as I learned, to *laugh through life.*

Tony Fonte is an intuitive and Reiki healer, a spiritual teacher, best-selling author, speaker, an entrepreneur, and the title he is most proud of, Dad. He helps those on a spiritual awakening healing journey break generational curses and become themselves, perhaps for the first time. He is a medium, which means he can intuitively channel Divine messages and then communicate those messages to his clients so that they can heal and let go of the trauma preventing them from creating the life of their dreams. Tony's spiritual gifts enable him to connect with the energy of others and know where they are storing their pain, so he can guide them in releasing or transmuting that energy. His greatest gift is using the frequency of laughter to help make the spiritual healing journey lighter. Healing can be fun! That is the core of the *Laughing Through Life Movement*, which Tony created.

www.tonyfonte.com/
linktr.ee/thetonyfonte

WHITNEY WISER

The Power of Proper Alignment

My body was broken and bruised. My dreams were crushed.

It was 2011. I was lying in a hospital bed as doctors told me I would have to learn how to walk again. I was told my competitive sports career was over, that I would not be able to compete in bodybuilding again, and that I should prepare myself for this new reality.

I was there because of someone who told me he loved me, just before he ran over me with his SUV. Let me back up to the beginning of my story.

I have always identified as an athlete. I played sports year-round every year from the age of nine all through high school and into college. As I was graduating from college, I had no idea what I was going to do with this important competitive athlete part of my life. Then I discovered bodybuilding.

I had no idea what I was getting myself into. I was reluctant as I started preparing for my first competition in 2009. Adapting to the new lifestyle was rough, but it didn't take long until I'd found a new love in the rigid, disciplined life of a competitor in the bodybuilding and fitness world.

After the rough start, I had my first show. Vowing never be outworked, I became very competitive, soon winning shows all over the country. Within two years, I was on my way to earning my pro status, which I never thought possible. I was getting nationwide recognition after winning two back-to-back national-level shows.

Then there was my personal life. I'd made the decision to get out of an abusive relationship just two weeks prior, but my ex-boyfriend wanted to talk. I agreed to meet him in the parking lot at my job.

It did not go well. The conversation ended with him running over me with his SUV. I was hit and got caught under the vehicle, dragged across the parking lot, and eventually crushed under the rear tire. He left me lying in the parking lot with a crushed spine, road burn all over my body, and struggling to breathe. I didn't know how badly I was injured, but the pain was excruciating. All I could do was to cry out to God to take the pain away.

Though seriously injured, I was coherent enough when emergency medical responders and police arrived to give a detailed description of my ex-boyfriend and his vehicle. State Troopers caught him speeding down the interstate. He was arrested and taken to jail.

I was transported to Vanderbilt Medical Center to have emergency back surgery. Metal rods and screws were fused into my spine, and I was then admitted into the Trauma Unit. After a week in the hospital, my mind still couldn't comprehend the extent of the injuries my body had endured. I remember being confused when my parents told me I would be coming to live with them for a while. I assumed I would be going back to my apartment. I didn't understand that I could not walk. After all, just a few days prior to this I was seemingly invincible...in my mind anyway.

In spite of the damage done to my body, my heart and mind were focused. There was no way I would give up on my dream of becoming a professional athlete. No one believed I would ever make it back to the stage, given the circumstances, but I wouldn't allow any doubt to enter my thoughts. I built a fortress around my mind to block out all doubt and negativity. Luckily, my God-given stubbornness (I like to call it resilience) was there for me, aiding me throughout my recovery.

Deep down, I knew I had to hold onto my hope and faith that God would redeem it all. I knew if I didn't stay positive, my spirit would die right along with my passion and dream. With no other option except to keep my faith that God would bring me through it, I was able to take both actual and imagined steps every day. I visualized myself back on stage daily as I walked countless laps around my parents' neighborhood block.

Recovery was hard and turned out to take much longer than I'd have liked, but by God's grace, one day at a time, I slowly built my body back and returned to the stage. Getting back on stage was only half the battle. I had some devastating defeats, but I never stopped pressing forward until I was competitive again. It took three years, but I was able to receive my pro status in the sport. I later went on to qualify and compete with the best pro athletes in the world on the Olympia stage in 2016. I didn't just accomplish my dream, I shot past it! That's how God works! We are capable of way more with Him than alone.

I had achieved it all…everything I'd ever wanted and more. But I knew I couldn't keep up with this highly competitive lifestyle forever. I was already involved in the sport as a judge, which I loved. I was also becoming increasingly bored with my career as a personal trainer. I didn't know what I wanted to do with my life or my powerful testimony. It appeared that I had it all looking from the outside in, but I was frustrated by my lack of direction. It also seemed like I lost my passion after accomplishing my life goal.

My career as a competitive athlete—what I had built my entire identity on—would have to end soon. I wasn't ready to face that reality, but while I struggled, I coached athletes on perfecting their posing and stage presence to show their physiques in the best way in order to win and be successful.

As I was leaving a posing session one day, I realized I wasn't just teaching these ladies how to pose. I was building their confidence by speaking life into them with encouraging words. Imagine getting on a stage and wearing almost nothing for your body to be judged and ranked among your peers. Not an easy thing to do. I began affirming them, helping them fight uncertainty with my extensive stage experience, leaving them with positive messages and strategies they could use. Helping them see who they really are and what they are capable of becoming (all the things we never see in ourselves) became my driving force.

A shift slowly started stirring. Up to that point, my purpose had only been about me. While coaching women who were all competing for their own reasons, I got to hear all their stories and motivation behind their decision to compete. Some were doing it to prove to themselves or someone else that they could.

Others used it as an outlet to overcome a bad relationship, a disease, a diagnosis. Whatever the reason, these women needed support, and I knew I could help.

That's when my focus shifted from myself to others. I'd gone from losing my identity to redefining my purpose. It was the most painful thing I'd ever done, more painful than learning how to walk again. Being able to help others, not in spite of but because of the pain I'd experienced, was therapeutic. It gave me what I needed to keep moving forward.

Over time, I started seeing how much was missing in the attention to detail and care of the athletes at local shows. These athletes trained really hard for months to do this, and I felt like the least they deserved was an amazing stage to walk out onto. They should be getting the experience of a lifetime, every time. From what I could see, it wasn't happening. Something needed to be done.

I got the idea to start an all-female bodybuilding and fitness competition. This hadn't been done successfully anywhere in the world—yet. I retired from competing in 2018 so I could focus on building an event specifically for women. The creation of the All-Female IFBB/NPC Nashville Fit Show was born out of a desire to give female athletes their own platform—a platform to promote women coming together to empower and support other women.

As the show expanded and I added other events, God started bringing more strong women into my life. So many women have come into my life, helping guide me over the years as mentors, coaches, friends, and clients. I love the quote, "If you want to go fast, go alone. But if you want to go far, go together!" I used to be a loner. Now I know our entire lives hinge on being aligned with the right people and having the right relationships! My events helped create this connection for women to be not just athletes but advocates to help build each other up in all areas of life. I call it the *power of proper alignment*, and I know it is the key to achieving the unique purpose we've each been called to fulfill.

Whitney Wiser has overcome what looks like insurmountable odds. Well on her way to the big leagues of competitive bodybuilding, she was run over and crushed by an SUV as a result of ending an abusive relationship. After having her spine fused back together and learning how to walk again, Whitney made her way not just back to bodybuilding but became a Pro Athlete and competed on the Olympia stage as one of the greatest fitness athletes in the world. Whitney went on to found Wiser Fitness in 2015 with the mission of empowering people to strengthen their body through nutrition and strength-training coaching. In 2017, she formed Fit Life Productions to host events and coaching on a wider scale to inspire confidence and strength in women. Her motto: "I believe without a doubt that with faith in God and a positive mindset, *we are all capable of anything.*"

www.Instagram.com/whitneywiserfit
www.Instagram.com/Nashvillefitshow
www.instagram.com/HerStyleEvents
www.instagram.com/wiserfitlife

KRISTEN SALVO

Fear is Fuel—Obstacles are Gifts

I was ten years old when I lost my mother to suicide.
She hung herself with the rope I was supposed to take to
Girl Scout camp that evening.

I was too young to understand discernment. What I did understand was shame, which I carried along with guilt, until I learned that shame and guilt are the lowest vibrations that one can embody.

Being ashamed of feelings is paralyzing. We are here to feel our way through this beautiful life, but too often we get attached to a story that is likely irrelevant in the present, or is false, becoming an obstacle that blocks the flow of life.

I have learned that I can stop the story and keep it from consuming the present moment. In its place, I have compassion and patience for myself as I move beyond to find freedom on the other side. This story is about finding that freedom.

Nothing is Permanent

It was difficult accessing the trauma I experienced at such a young age. I did a great job covering it up and avoiding it. I didn't have the proper support, so it turned into a constant internal battle.

Then, three years after losing my mom, I found a hidden camera in my private space, placed there by a loved one. I exposed him and the camera, but it was swept under the rug, and I was left to deal with this emotionally on my own. Having to pretend that it didn't happen left me feeling alone and afraid of everyone around me. The only one I felt safest with was my grandmother, my mother's mother, and I was told that I couldn't tell her what happened.

In August 2011, my sweet grandmother went into the hospital. She had stage-four lung cancer and only twelve months to live, at most.

Once again, my world came crashing down. A year later, her long, hard battle ended, and I felt like I had lost my only unconditional love and safety. With her gone, I was truly lost.

Two months after my grandmother passed, I met a woman who saw my pain. It resonated with her, and she shared different healing modalities with me that had helped her. She also helped me see I had to take the first step to heal myself.

That first step was really difficult. On April 1, 2013, I stood in front of a building in south St. Louis, sick to my stomach, afraid to enter. I'd promised myself that I would take this step, so I did. This was my first Al-Anon meeting. Al-Anon is a free, worldwide support group for survivors of dysfunction. I went to three-hundred-and-sixty-five meetings, obtained a sponsor, and worked the steps. The most significant benefit was that I finally had the support I needed to open up and be vulnerable with my trauma. I learned I was not alone, my trauma was real, and the answer was *support*! The door to my awareness opened. Deep healing was possible.

Ready to go deeper, I decided to fly to Joshua Tree, California, to sit with a world-renowned meditation teacher, Jack Kornfield. I'd never meditated a day in my life, but the opportunity *felt* so good, I signed up to sit alone, with no eye contact, no talking, and no cell phones for ten days. I didn't know how I was going to do it, but I knew it was the right thing at the right time.

On day three, struggling, I went for a walk, sat on a bench that overlooked Joshua Tree National Park, and said to the wind, "How in the world did I manage to get here?"

Waiting for the answer, I felt a quiet peace within and around me, something I'd never experienced. Overwhelmed with gratitude, I then felt a presence wrapping around me like a blanket. I quickly realized that my mother and grandmother were there with me.

My question was answered. I was there to learn there is more to life than what can be seen. I was no longer alone. I was safe. I had guides on the other side.

This experience taught me that obstacles aren't something to run from but to lean into. I've since learned that obstacles are where our gifts are hidden, and we only find those gifts when we get clear on why something has become an obstacle. Even fear can become fuel for healing. Pushing through fear allowed me to learn more about myself and explore what was on the other side. It took years of attending retreats, starting relationships, and tortured endings, feeling lost and inadequate, like I could never be enough. Each trauma took me back into deep suffering, the place where, as a child, I would go into my closet and cry out to God, "Why did you give me this life so full of obstacles?"

Then I realized none of this was God's fault. Having lost my healing center, I was now only reacting to things — unable to access answers. Change was needed. I was blocked!

The Signs

October 2020, I was back in a place where I felt blocked. Searching for answers, a friend recommended that I visit Sedona, Arizona. I looked it up and immediately felt called to go but decided to put it in my back pocket for a later date. Two days later I received an email from a tribe that I had sat with on a retreat in Costa Rica, inviting me to sit with them and drink ayahuasca in Sedona. I knew instantly that this was my sign to accept this opportunity. I immediately called them and told them that I would be there.

When I got on the plane a few weeks later, I was ready to completely surrender the things that held me back and be open to receive the beautiful wisdom and lessons that I needed to step into my power. I read *The Four Agreements* on my flight, which supported the intention that I had. I landed in Flagstaff and drove forty minutes to Sedona. The drive there was healing in itself. I was overcome with emotions and the energy emanating from the red-rock formations, as if the land embraced me.

I spent a few days exploring the land both alone and with different healers. The most profound session I had was with a native healer who took me to his sacred place on top of a hill that overlooked the most stunning parts of Sedona. His healing teachings were unusual, and I didn't completely understand the healing that I was supposed to be receiving, but I went along with it, my heart and mind open. At the end of the session, he told me he wanted to take a photo of me on top of this hill with the red rocks in the background. I carefully worked my way out to the edge to ensure that the photo captured all that surrounded me. He asked me to put my arms out wide like an eagle spreading its wings. It was liberating. I heard him say, "Stand still. There is an orb coming from the sky and it is heading towards you." In that instant, I remembered getting a massage in 2013 from a reiki master, during which I received a vision of myself on top of a mountain with my arms spread wide, happy and at peace. My only reference then was the mountain that I had hiked in Big Sur, California, at a meditation retreat. At this moment in Sedona, I finally understood the vision.

It was of my highest and best self at the time of self-discovery. I couldn't believe what was happening, but I knew to stay grounded and enjoy all of the beauty that I felt within and around me. That evening I went into ceremony with clear intention. I told the Tiata, the native shaman, that I wanted to *see my gifts*, meaning I wanted to see all parts of me and my potential. He blew the prayer into the cup, and I proceeded to drink the medicine.

That evening my life changed forever. I received clarity and wisdom that would carry me into the version of myself that I was striving to be. But the greatest gift was the connection with my mom. My mom came to me and showed me a porcelain Native American doll and even showed me where it was in my house. I didn't know if this was real or true. It felt like it.

When I arrived home, I went straight to the storage area and pulled out the tub that she showed me in my vision. The doll was on top. Loud and clear, the message to me was that there is more to life than what I can see, and that I am divinely guided and protected. I didn't need to be scared anymore. I kept digging in the tub and found letters, treasures, and guidance that she had left for me, things that aligned perfectly with the journey I was on. These items were a clear indication that my mom did not leave me. She prepared and exited so that she could guide me from the other side to help ease me out of the suffering passed down to me through generational trauma, trauma that was unresolved due to lack of support. My mom was there with me and still is to this day.

By opening up about my experiences and connecting with amazing humans, I received healing. There is so much beauty and healing in connection, vulnerability, and unconditional love. My story grows exponentially from here. Today I live in Sedona and share the healing and wisdom that I have received with those who are truly ready to surrender and receive. I remind myself and others that this journey of life requires aligning ourselves with people, places, and things that bring meaning, grace, and love to ourselves.

Life is happening *for* us, not *to* us. I use this mantra on a daily basis. It reminds me to look at the gift in everything in life. From a young age, my family would get so sick of hearing me saying, "it's a sign," but it truly is, and those who are open to it are the ones that will receive. My success, challenges, breakthroughs, and opportunities are all gifts that I have been given, and I have learned that if greed or doubt start to seep in, those blessings will quickly stop, and I will then be given another lesson to learn.

I know the importance of believing there is hope within each of us, and the moment that we lose hope, it is a reminder that it is time to Shift with Intention. To shift out of the comfort zone and dive into the unknown. This zone of the unknown offers humility, faith, love, support, and, more importantly, *happiness*. Staying in comfort, it is easy to get depressed and stagnant. We must take risks in order to grow. Remember that life really is on your side and that support is the main ingredient for growth.

To be continued…

Kristen Salvo started her still-successful career as an entrepreneur when she was eighteen years old, her drive fueled by fear. In 2013, a traumatic experience motivated her to search for life's deeper meaning. Her quest has taken her to jungles where she drank ayahuasca with indigenous tribes, and to Joshua Tree where she spent thirty days in silent meditation with world-renowned leaders. She's spent countless hours with life coaches, and has applied her laser-beam focus on nutrition and exercise. With a burning desire to help others on this journey, she learned alternative healing modalities outside the Western approach, applying them to first heal her deep wounds and then to teach others how to turn *fear into fuel and obstacles into opportunities*. She resides in Sedona, Arizona, and believes that a balanced life of faith, support, love, and passion are the ingredients needed to manifest a life beyond our wildest dreams.

www.facebook.com/kristen.salvo.5

It Doesn't Have to Be This Way

Life can only be understood backwards; but it must be lived forwards.

–Søren Kierkegaard

I was sitting in the passenger seat of a pickup truck going over a country road in Illinois when my buddy looked at me and asked me if I'd go to church with him. As a licensed therapist, I can't advocate for any one particular religion over another, but I can tell you how I responded on that day twenty-two years ago. "Well, clearly what I've been doing doesn't work, so I guess I'm open to trying something different."

You don't have to go to church to change your life. But you do need to do something different than you've ever done before if you want to see different results. When I agreed to go with my buddy to his church on Sunday, riding shotgun on the bumpy backroads of Illinois, I was far from being a master of my circumstance. To put it plainly, I was lost.

Twenty-nine years old, an inch from filing for bankruptcy, divorced not once, not twice, but three strikes you're out, and fired from more jobs than the number of years I'd been alive. It wouldn't be a stretch to say that I was a wreck of a human being. I needed a change, and for me, showing up at church was the much-needed answer to my proverbial prayers.

If you are reading this book, you may have a few doubts about the circumstances comprising your own life right now. The question you have to ask yourself is this: *Is what you are doing getting you what you want out of life?* My guess is that it's not. I have some good news for you, though. *It doesn't have to be this way.*

I've learned as a therapist that every person who walks into my counseling practice carries a slight feeling of existential despair. (I know what you're thinking—*this guy turned out to be a therapist?* Actually, being a horrible person and overcoming your own crap can make you pretty good at helping other people with theirs. It also pays a lot better than working at Gitcho's Gas Station.)

In some clients, existential despair is very subtle, almost imperceptible. In others, it's written on their sleeve for everyone in their life to see—except for them. No matter who we are or what we do, there's an uncertainty hiding within us all about what our purpose is and how we can live the lives we were meant to lead.

Now, the type of despair I'm talking about doesn't necessarily involve a lot of sulking and crying. It's more of an unconscious habit, or something *we've just accepted as the way things are.* For a long time in my life, I just accepted my bad attitude, my ability to get fired from jobs, to blow up relationships, and to *torch* bridges. It was just who I was. *That's just the way it is* might as well have been written down in my will as what should go on my tombstone. However, the more I worked through those unconscious habits and thoughts, the more I realized that I wasn't excited about my life, and my boredom caused me to search out trouble. Then I discovered I had other choices.

Becoming a Force of Nature

Marcus Aurelius wrote in *Meditations*: "People who love what they do wear themselves down doing it, they even forget to wash or eat." George Bernard Shaw is known to have said, "This is the true joy in life, the being used for a purpose recognized by yourself as a mighty one; the being thoroughly worn out before you are thrown on the scrap heap; the being a force of Nature instead of a feverish selfish little clod of ailments and grievances complaining that the world will not devote itself to making you happy."

These quotes sum up the tension between what we want our lives to look like versus our fear of change and facing what we don't know. Mystery and the unknown permeate everything we do in life, even though we may not be able to recognize them consciously. If we can't pinpoint this angst for what it is, it continues to go undiagnosed, allowing uncertainty to eventually seep into our relationships, our careers, and our personal aspirations. We quickly learn to cover this up. And the better we get at covering it up, the more it masks our true potential from shining through.

Take it from me; I was virtually unemployable, undatable, and unapologetic about being a jerk about all of it. Today, I run a business that supports several families, including my own. To get to where I am today, I had to dig deep, deeper than I ever had before and start asking the really hard questions.

"Does it really have to be this way?"

I was sick of resigning myself to a replay of the movie *Groundhog Day*. Every day was an endless loop of me doing the same stupid stuff to sabotage my life, all while thinking that *something outside of me was going to change me*. Many of us living in the world today are like I was—resistant to change. We wake up every morning and do the same things without even thinking, living on autopilot.

Hard Truths

There's a hard truth we must learn at some point in our lives: *we can't control our circumstances, but we can control ourselves.* In order to do this, we have to remove the resistance, the *"it is what it is"* mentality, because at its core, all that is, is an excuse.

You know it. That false sense of acceptance that is holding you back from getting where you want to go. Here's another hard truth: *you have to let go of your attachment to the outcome before you can truly own your actions.*

And yet another truth: *you can do everything perfectly and still jack it all up.* For instance, you can drink gallons of freshly squeezed carrot juice for breakfast, run five miles a day, never smoke, never touch a drop of alcohol, be in bed by 9:30 p.m., live a stress-free life, and still die a horribly painful battle to cancer. I'm not being flippant; I'm being realistic.

There's a greater philosophical truth at work that doesn't consider how many pull-ups you can do, or how high your cholesterol is: *meaning can only be derived from your own choices and how you feel about them.* I'm not saying to neglect your health and be Keith Richards—although Keith Richards seems pretty happy—I'm saying that all you can control is the way you act in the world. You don't get to choose how it impacts the world around you.

So, what does that mean? It means that you can't control what happens to you, the circumstances that you're thrown into, no matter what you do. However, even though cause and effect isn't always a perfect 100 percent matchup from expectation to reality, they do add up most of the time. For example, how many smokers have you heard of who died of lung cancer? Probably quite a few. It may not mean that you will get cancer, but it increases the likelihood. Similarly, there are probably a lot of *illusions* that you are living with that keep you blind to what is really going on in your heart, in your head, and in your interactions with the outside world. In my book, *Master of Circumstance*, the goal was to elucidate the ways you are diminishing your chances of mastery, and how you can maximize your outcome so that you get the best shot at living masterfully.

As I was recording the audio book version of *Master of Circumstance*, something new occurred to me. I had read that book cover to cover over twenty times as I edited and re-edited it to turn it into the final product. What I noticed while reading it this time is that two things were needed to *stop being a victim* and really start the process of *becoming Master of Circumstance*: 1) full acceptance of where you are right now, and 2) forgiveness of both those who guided you into this place and yourself for staying here.

I was working out the other morning while listening to a podcast from Jordan Peterson. He is one of my favorite authors and speakers on the subject of mindset and living well. When discussing acceptance, of really looking at acceptance of where you are and *who* you are, *right now*, a question needs to be asked. Are you ready to feel punched in the gut and face yourself honestly, to be more honest than you have ever been? Here's the question you need to ask: "What am I doing to completely screw up my life?"

A Place of Acceptance

Come on, you know the answers to this question. When you are honest about the answers and you are serious about your introspection, you will arrive at a different place, a place of *acceptance*. Once you hit acceptance, you will have access to something new. You will have access to a way out. You will have access to what it is you really need to do that will *shift* your life forever.

The Road of Forgiveness

In order to take the answers that you produce and really make a difference, you will now have to travel down the road of forgiveness. There is a feeling that shows up with unforgiveness, a bitterness, a resentment that is always under the surface. It's not just toward the person who hurt you. It's a lump that is embedded in your gut. To remove it, you have to commit to setting all that bitterness and resentment aside, and then move forward.

It's important to understand this about forgiveness: it isn't just a one-time thing. Forgiveness is an all-the-time thing, like a skin you put on. You have to forgive again and again, until it finally sticks, and then when it undoubtedly rears its ugly head, you will have to forgive again.

Forgiveness doesn't mean that we make what happened OK, or that we agree with another's position. It doesn't mean that others don't have to face the consequences of their actions or words. It doesn't mean reconciliation or restoration. All forgiveness means is that you are not going to hold what happened against the person any longer. That's all it means; nothing more, nothing less.

When you accept that the past is just the past, that it was a lesson you can learn from, *then* allow yourself to forgive those who hurt you, and finally be able forgive yourself for being defined by and staying in a hurtful place for too long— once you do these things, then you are *free* to move forward with *power in and over your life.*

James (Jamie) Morgan completed his master's degree in professional counseling in 2013 and started his private practice in January of 2014. He currently serves as the president and clinical director of My Family Counseling, Inc, a group mental-health practice he and his wife formed in July 2017. After graduating high school in 1989, Jamie joined the US Navy, serving as an air traffic controller. When he left the Navy in 1994, he started a construction company and has been in some construction related businesses most of his life, as well as being an entrepreneur. My Family Counseling is his passion as he creates generational wealth and a legacy of excellence with his business model. Jamie is a published author, with his debut book, Master of Circumstance, as well as a podcaster. Jamie and Sandra have been married for twenty years this April and share ownership in the S-Corp.

www.myfcinc.com
www.masterofcircumstance.com

The Common Denominator

If you do not tell the truth about yourself,
you cannot tell the truth about other people.

– Virginia Woolf

*H*eart pounding like it wants out. Can't breathe, think, or see. I'm on the side of the road, in my truck, but don't know where. Fuck! My eyes burn and thoughts won't form. I try to call for help, but the phone is too complicated. I collapse against the steering wheel. I don't want to be me. Suicide is too complex to even consider. I am alone, hurt, terrified, with nowhere to go.

Why does this keep happening? Why do I attract abusive people? Why won't they love me?

My breathing returns to normal, my eyes focus, and my head clears. Something's different. I'm broken, yes, but something is different. I'm aware. I understand. Until I ensure this monster cannot find me, this will never stop. I am the one who must stop this.

My abuser, we will call X:
- knew I was molested by family and later raped, but did nothing.
- called me fat, ugly, and unworthy daily.
- fed me food, void of nutrition, year after year, demanding I work harder and harder.
- reminded me often how gross I was, sickened by the sight of me.
- put me dead last for recognition or support.

- broke every promise made to me.
- forced me to have sex with vile humans who lied, hit, verbally abused, gaslit, stole from, and intimidated me, shaming me mercilessly afterward.
- refused to get me help to care for my high-need child.
- refused to let me sleep or take a day off.
- poisoned my cup, my plate, my lungs, and my body with toxic doses until I no longer cared.

The torture escalated until I saw X for who she really was. Sitting there, in that truck, I realized the common denominator.

I was X.

"They" didn't hurt me. I fucking allowed it. I would fight anyone who treated my son the way I allowed others to treat *me*. I did this. I overlooked, excused, and created a self-inflicted prison, ripe for abuse. I was easily the most abusive of all who "loved" me. I never protected, fed, spoke to, or cared for myself with any kind of love. I looked for someone, out there, to "properly" love me, while privately, brutally bullying myself, sending worthy candidates to the curb for the slightest violation of my "rules," under the veil of protecting myself from *their* bullshit.

My amateur parents taught me an extensive list of don't-face-your-emotions concoctions: food, drink, things, activities, even sexual abuse. This was how I loved myself and felt loved. Abuse had always been my bar. No wonder things were fucked up.

I chose habitual abuse, creatively manifested. Too lazy to do the leg work, I found others to help. Tired of getting hit, I would go for verbal or sexual abuse, narcissism, or gaslighting, and when no one was available, I'd use food, substances, and rigid diets to make sure the abuse was consistent. Each time, proclaiming never again to submit to that *exact flavor of abuse*. It could be anyone: my lover, friend, employee, or random person. I was an equal opportunity abusee.

But, if X wasn't to be in charge again, who was?

Was I? That seemed dangerous. Didn't I just determine I did this in the first place?

I knew X. We had predictable, although painful, patterns.

Why couldn't I be loved? Could I love? No matter who I dated, it started and ended the same. If they treated me slightly less like shit than I did, I assumed it was love. I worked to *keep* my abuser. My internal bully needed a friend. My victim needed to finally "make it work" with someone.

Then I had that moment in my truck. Nothing was out there. No one was out there. It was all inside of me. It was time to fall in love with myself and *know* the feeling.

Society made loving yourself look fun and shiny, in happy hours and pedicures. When I started reviewing how I love, I confused items of survival—like a nap, phone call, or meal—as a self-love reward. I had no notion of unconditional love of self.

I finally discovered self-love in the quiet, alone hours—no distractions, just me and my thoughts, taking the time to process and evaluate each one for validity. I got to know my lover honestly this time. To know a present, attentive, trusted lover, I needed time with her. I had to be vulnerable, and it was ugly. And beautiful. That is where intimacy begins, being patient through the ugly parts. It took discipline to love away my rigid rules of imagined protection. It took honesty.

My prior misconceptions about love allowed me to easily attract other abusive energy. Misery does love company. Removing myself from that broken dating pool, I had control of *me*. I would love myself in every interaction with my body now. This took commitment. Failure would have been an easy, not-loving route. I chose love even—and especially—when I didn't want to.

How could I know love unless I loved myself? I asked for unconditional love from "them" with a bucketload of conditions. Who could touch me and love every inch the way I craved if I didn't know what it felt like? Who inspires or maneuvers my rules of love if not me? How will they know me if I don't?

More important, why should they if I won't?

I now love myself unconditionally, so I know what unconditional love *feels* like. I apologize if I have made this sound warm and fuzzy; it is certainly not. Loving a toddler requires patience and oodles of self-control. They must be disappointed daily to grow, or it's being done the wrong way. Their absolute mission is to explore in wonder, versus ours, which is to guide, love, and keep them safe. I love myself enough to apply the same rules I know instinctually to apply to a toddler so that I can avoid those unpleasant tantrums in myself. They are called boundaries.

My options:

- My Creator says, I've given you Self. Take care of her as you believe I would. Love her, feed her, protect her, teach her how to give and receive love. I gave you instinct and every food. This is your sole purpose. *Love* her unconditionally. Give her the healthiest, most joyful life. Regardless of what she does, lovingly guide and teach her. Anything else you do will need to be in addition to *this* role.

Or

- I tell my Creator that I can't love her unconditionally and protect her because I met a hot guy and his excuses are different this time, it seems hard, I don't like confrontation, and the process sounds uncomfortable. I prefer to allow myself and others to treat this precious being poorly.

Which do I accept? Eventually, I accepted the first option. It wasn't easy.

In addition to the normal mix of children, I was given (or accepted, depending how you believe) a special child to care for along with the business of caring for me. He's now in his twenties, is developmentally a six-month old infant, bedridden, and has shown me (please don't let me make this sound easy either) the meaning of loving unconditionally. I fight for his existence...every...single...day.

Finally, I understood the assignment. It took twenty-three years before I realized that I am lovingly obliged to do the same and nothing less for myself. I had been caught up in distractions. I was sad, bored, frustrated. I avoided loving/healing myself. Happily, I am done with that shit now!

Loving and trusting myself took time, arduous work, and absolute prioritization. I had to forgive all of me and demand love, every instant. The repairs and recovery were uncomfortable, and I did crazy shit to avoid the work that was required. So, I resisted and persisted.

I lovingly manage my toddler heart, daily, sometimes minute-by-minute, to keep on track. Even now, when I try to act out, I love me, stop me, and correct me, lovingly.

I hold myself to the Highest Standard of Loving Me and set the bar for how I dare to be loved, (so the Universe fulfills). The only way to get the love I crave, is to set *my bar*. This focused, loving, discipline exponentially drove the process. I became lovingly firm.

Who had a great laugh, stance, outlook, mood? Who picked the most nutritious foods, smiled the most, was the most dependable? I inquired about love everywhere I went, with everyone. What do they eat? How do they get organized, apply discipline, create routines? To what do they attribute their amazing attitude?

My mind and heart opened to new ways to experience love. Opportunities to love myself were unlimited. I had been playing so small in love. I was now able to play bigger in *love!*

Who could be more honest with me than me? No one else has all the information to fact-check. But I hadn't been keeping my word to myself. I had ignored those feelings of chaos, frustration, and confusion that I now know tell me when I'm on the wrong track . . . even when I don't want that to be the case. I got honest! I lovingly hold myself accountable. I listen to myself. (Again, don't confuse honesty with nice or pleasant; it's scary and difficult.)

I am still learning about this *love* stuff. The things I don't know are exciting because it means I have only begun to experience love! I listen to the words I say and think. Honesty allows me to change my mind about things that don't serve me or weren't even mine! When I am honest, I'm in control of how my body moves, feels, and experiences being in love. Once I open myself to new ideas, I grow, I blossom!

Before I could know the touch of someone who loved every aspect of me, I had to recognize it. I was and am my only possible example. I *love* me now. I trust I will protect myself from a place of love. I honestly decide if I am doing the best for my mind and body. I know when and if I feel love. It's really this simple. Love is more than spoken; it is emotion and energy, harmony, and intent. I have learned to detect it when I love myself with no one looking. When I lovingly keep myself safe and growing, even when it is momentarily uncomfortable. When I speak only lovingly to myself and attract the unconditional, love I give. These are the commitments that allow me to do so safely.

I have exclusive, full audience to all of me, every thought. I am still the common denominator, only now I know *the language of the love of the one person who knows everything about me.* I know I am not my body, my arms, my messy bathroom, past traumas, job, or anything anyone ever said about or done to me. The loving *me* knows this and has control. I am in charge. This allows the little girl I am to protect, to flourish, and to experience the entirety of love in the full protection of *me*! With each new discovery, I deconstruct any imaginary, abusive, expired thoughts and recreate them from love.

I am in my badass truck. My hands are firmly on the wheel. The windows are down, the music is up, and sunlight warms my face while my long hair blows where it chooses. I am madly in love and taking myself wherever the hell I want to go. Love surrounds me everywhere. It's safe now. I am there to protect myself. I have become the love of my dreams! And I am thankful there is so much more to learn.

Misti retired as CEO at the onset of the pandemic to care for her disabled son, who is one of her four biological children, four stepchildren, twenty-nine exchange students, and three who stopped by for a spell. After significant downsizing, Misti and Hayden live in a secluded, unassuming, free-range spot in southeast Oklahoma. Misti spends her days loving: herself, her son, their plants, animals, and the planet. She coordinates and is growing an organic community garden and building a campground where others can experience the beauty of healing in nature. Since 1995, she has mentored those who wish to address addictions, change behaviors, body shape, and improve life by removing their perceived limitations. She believes life is about possibilities and shares her passion for the freedom that comes with love and *joy*. She can be followed at "Living Without Labels With Misti" on Facebook.

www.facebook.com/labelfreeliving

Is It a Habit or a Choice?

Should I stay? Should I leave? What about the kids?

I was raised in a Christian home where divorce was frowned upon. Still, I was unhappy and couldn't find much good in my relationship. I wasn't giving and I wasn't getting what I needed to feel loved and fulfilled. We had been married for seventeen years and I had been happy, but we got to a point where I just fell out of love. I wanted to keep our family together, but I couldn't imagine living the rest of my life feeling sad, unloved, and wondering how I could ever find inner peace and joy again. I felt like a failure.

I had just started a new business and was going out of town for a weekend to a conference. Before I left, I told my husband that I didn't love him anymore, that I had been feeling like this for quite a while, and that something needed to change. I told him I wasn't sure I wanted to stay in the marriage.

While at my conference, I met a couple of women who I believe were there by divine intervention. We bonded quickly, and in the three days we were together, we had deep conversations about relationships. I shared my feelings and situation and was encouraged to not give up, but to seek counsel and see if things could change for the better. One of those women had left her relationship and said, "It's not always greener on the other side." She had regrets. The other told me about her marital hardships in the past, how they overcame them, and how they were happier than they had ever been.

When I returned home very late one night, my oldest daughter, then in high school, was waiting up for me in the kitchen. Old enough to know what was going on, she begged me not to leave. She pleaded with me to try anything I could to stay and be happy. After the encouragement from my new friends at the conference and my daughter begging me to stay, I decided to look for a counselor, anticipating we would need to have marriage counseling together. This was not easy for me. It was clear I had to shift something inside myself to even want to try to mend my marriage. I had given up, which meant I had to work on myself separately as well.

I went to a therapist who'd come highly recommended. I only saw her a few times, but what I got from her was profound. It started a shift in me that literally changed my life! She assured me that I was not the only woman who has ever been in this situation and that there was nothing wrong with me. She told me to write down the top three qualities in my husband that I loved. Then she told me whenever I had a negative thought about him (which was all the time), to think of these three qualities. The objective was to remind me why I had loved my husband in the past.

That's when I noticed my thoughts were often negative, that it was easier to judge and find something wrong with other people than it was to change myself! I began wondering why it was so much easier to think negatively than positively. That didn't make sense.

So, I told myself: "I do want to try and make this work. I want to love him again. I want to keep our little family together."

And that is what I did. Every time I had a negative thought about him, I reminded myself of the top three reasons I fell in love with him. To my amazement, my feelings shifted. I was starting to see the good in him again. He took me on a date just weeks after I began this new habit, and I had butterflies again! It was one of the most memorable dates we have ever had. I saw what a simple shift in mindset could do. I was falling in love with him again and it was the greatest feeling in the world. There was passion and desire again! It didn't happen overnight, but it kept happening because I was so intentional about what I was thinking. I was committed to only having positive thoughts and to see the good.

It worked!

Granted, he knew how I was feeling prior to this, and he was trying to give me what I needed. What else changed? Well, instead of thinking only about myself and what I needed, I realized I needed to give him what he needed. Sounds so simple. It is!

We had counseling sessions and read a marriage book together, which had conversation exercises that were recommended after each chapter. This book offered advice on communication and how to shift your thoughts to the qualities you love about your spouse instead of focusing on the negative. When we both started focusing on the positive aspects of each other, our love deepened. I can say today that I have never loved him more than I do right now!

I could have given up and left. I didn't have to try to save our marriage, but the encouragement from new friends and my daughter ignited the desire to salvage my marriage. If I had the chance to keep my family together, I wanted to. It was not an easy road, and it took both of us shifting our mindset. Thinking positively literally saved my marriage.

Then it changed my life. Having seen how powerful positive thinking had been for our relationship, I decided to start thinking positively about other things. It's easy to focus on negative thoughts, not by choice but by habit. I began saying affirmations to myself instead of complaining about what I didn't like about me. I started feeling more confident. I started thinking about the good in people who I was around, a real shift from the easy way I'd seen the negative in them. My relationships deepened. I started to see the good in daily situations and hardships instead of complaining all day long. I became an all-around happier woman. I started to feel an inner peace, which led me to deepen my spiritual life, to not be angry and crabby all the time, and really to think of others in a brighter light. I started to be grateful for everything. Everything! It was an intentional shift in my mindset. It is as simple as it sounds, but our minds are so accustomed to finding fault, complaining, and being negative, it takes focused effort to reverse that habit. To consciously think positively.

I recommend it. It's going to take time and effort. It may take daily journaling, which I did regularly, or Post-it Notes around the house or desk, reminders on your phone or calls from friends to keep you accountable, but shifting your mindset is achievable. It's a habit. The older the habit, the harder it is to break; but with perseverance and determination, a mindset can be changed, and, in turn, life can change.

Of all the choices I could have made, I chose my husband. I chose my family, I chose to change my entire way of thinking, and, ultimately, I changed my life. It really was as simple as intentionally and repeatedly thinking of the three things I loved most about my spouse. This turned into intentionally and repeatedly thinking of what I loved and what was good about my friends, my family, my unwanted circumstances, and my day-to-day happenings—about myself.

My advice? Do it! Form a habit. Practice. Be grateful, see the good. Be intentional. Surround yourself with people who are positive and lift you up. Your whole perspective can change, just like mine did.

Don't get me wrong, I still have plenty of moments when my mind wants to divert and go back to old habits, but I recognize the pattern. Three steps: first, recognize habitual responses; second, change them; and third, keep changing them until the new, positive habit becomes more natural than the old, negative habit. You get to choose!

April Abbonizio is a Certified Advanced Clinical Thermographer at Midwest Thermography Solutions in Towne and Country, Missouri. She believes living a healthy lifestyle starts with information and prevention, and that thermography is a cornerstone for both. Formerly a dental hygienist, she experienced health issues that were resolved by changing her diet, lifestyle, and healing naturally. April attended the Institute for Integrative Nutrition and became a board-certified integrative nutrition health coach. Shortly after starting that business, she learned about thermography and became fascinated with the safety, early detection, and efficacy of thermal imaging. She incorporated thermography into her practice and became certified through the American College of Clinical Thermology. Her passion is guiding patients to optimal health through the use of thermography, health coaching, providing with report consultations, resources, and referrals so each patient receives the information and opportunity needed to achieve optimal health.

www.midwestthermographysolutions.com
www.facebook.com/midwestthermographysolutions
info@midwesttherm.com

A Designed Life

I am a powerful, confident, choice-filled, healthy woman.

I didn't always know or identify with all of those words. It took a series of events, years of learning and self-discovery, introspection, and practice, practice, practice.

The first significant shift and intention was to go on a six-week architectural study/tour of Europe my junior year of college. The shift was the first time I decided to choose something without getting my parents' blessing. Having been tremendously supported throughout my life, this was outside my comfort zone. I did not know then that this decision would set me on a lifetime course of shifting with intention. This became the roadmap for the rest of my life.

I wasn't the student with overflowing buckets of money during college. Or at least, this was my perspective. I was frugal to the point of not having fun. I didn't go out or feel like I could take part in activities because my *mindset was focused on scarcity*. I was about to realize how the universe responds when you are clear and move forward *as if*.

Three payments were required throughout the year for the trip. My student loan was unexpectedly increased. I never knew how I was going to make the next payment, yet the money showed up. For instance, my parents' friends from church secretly sent me money because they heard I was operating on faith and they wanted to support my faith in action.

Completing the payments and studying abroad were the keys I needed to solidify my understanding around setting intentions.

I graduated college during the recession. I thought I was ready for the world and all it had to offer. However, I did not get the interior design job in St. Louis that year.

Little did I know my shift would be to "sit quietly" for one year in a small town in Southern Illinois working in the office at a factory. During this year of quiet, I strengthened my belief system, listened, journaled, and set my next intentions to move to St. Louis and meet my Mr. Right.

I gained clarity and set my intention by typing a list of one hundred characteristics my Mr. Right would embody. He found me nine months later, still two-and-a-half hours away from St. Louis in that small town.

He told me later that what attracted him to me was my goal setting. He saw my calendar with appointments including the day I would start my new job as an interior designer, move to St. Louis, turn on my utilities, and celebrate my achievements. All of those dates were intentions set three months in the future but already documented in my calendar. As it turned out, all of those events happened two weeks later than my predetermined goals. Still, it was a strong start. I was now addicted to stretching my beliefs, my growth, and my faith in what was possible.

Intentions became part of my everyday practice, and I have sustained them over the last thirty years. My shift was from powerless to powerful, from having no choice to being choice-filled, and from low self-image to being confident in my purpose. The most challenging and lengthy shift in my life has been going from a mindset of scarcity of time and money to an abundance mentality.

Fast-forward to lockdown in March of 2020, which kicked off a completely new shift in my life. Being home and working from home full time with a group of grown-up, adult children had its challenges and blessings. The tension with my husband was at an all-time high because I was so miserable and stressed by my job.

This shift happened when I was encouraged to take a three-day silent, fasting retreat at a hermitage near our home. I thought this was one of the craziest ideas I had ever heard, but in August of 2020, I drove to the country, keeping my expectations low, my self-talk keeping me humble. "What if I didn't hear what I wanted? What if I didn't hear anything? Can you actually fail at retreating?" I began with gratitude, even though I wasn't feeling grateful at that time. After all, I was here because I was at a loss and didn't know my next steps.

On day one I read The Noticer by Andy Andrews and took notes on life lessons about perspective, worry, gratitude, discernment, wisdom, hope, abundance, success, choice, self-reflection and time.

Day two I read *You Are the Girl for the Job* by Jess Connolly. Another day of notes about how I am perfectly enabled to do the job that I was called to do in this life, for the joy and the blessing of those around me at this appointed time.

That was a much larger perspective than I had while I was in my small-minded pity-party mode. As I continued to sit in silence, I stopped resisting and realized that health in all forms was my priority.

On August 14, 2020, I declared and wrote out my next intention on a piece of torn, trace paper. What I Want: Healthy workspace, EOS culture, clean processes, clarity of purpose, respect, genuine appreciation, engagement in the business, no game playing, thriving team with growth plans identified, autonomous and trusted to make decisions for my team, exceptions are exceptions and not the rule, valued as an expert and asset to the company, culture of giving back, doesn't daily hurt my soul, honors my thought process, room to be authentic, healthy boundaries, listened to (heard), true leadership from executives, room for growth, do what is right, intentional sales goals and measurables, love coming in every day, stay the course, teamwork, brainstorm, openness to others' ideas and acceptance if the final direction isn't my top choice, ability to speak the truth from my perspective.

Yes, all of that on one piece of trace paper, a list of all the things that were not present at that moment. Was it even possible to find the healthy workspace I was envisioning? Was I asking too much? Did I deserve all of those things listed? What was the next step? Where was this place I was searching for and how would I find it?

While creating a list of potential career options for the next chapter of my trace-paper career, I decided there were no limits and no bad ideas. I thoroughly researched five consultancy businesses. I entertained creating my own position at my husband's company (I did not get that job). The list even included Eat, Pray,

Love and become a Starbucks barista at Target to reduce the stress and anxiety in my life. I listed all of the pros and cons for each.

Next, I created a resume, reached out to experts associated for each business I investigated. I created an Excel spreadsheet showing financial comparisons with earning potential over the next ten years to determine if we would need to downsize our life. I created a budget that limited our spending to ensure I wouldn't send us into financial ruin or prevent us from retirement. I met with my husband and other mentors to vet my ideas.

If I was open to a drastic lifestyle and financial change to improve my health, I planned on being prepared. My intention was to walk away from a thirty-year career to completely shift my focus and life toward health in all forms. Interesting how this intent was so strong it foreshadows the next series of events. While continuing to pursue other options, I kept my head in the game and stayed engaged in my position because I loved the people and the challenge of leadership. If I was leaving, I was determined to leave well.

Sitting up in bed one evening, I had a pivotal moment. I said to my husband, "I am good at this! Why should I have to leave?"

What I decided at that moment was to create the healthy space I'd envisioned on the trace paper at my current company. How would that even be possible? I have learned that change starts inside ourselves. So, I focused on the things I was able to influence. I enjoyed being home at five during lockdown to start dinner early. I found gratitude in small hidden places, like being able to walk at lunch and having animals in the office at home all day.

There was a small but growing glimmer of the trace-paper career I declared in order to save my health in 2020. By August 1, 2021, we were implementing the strategies from the trace paper. The company was starting its transition, and the leadership was excited about what was to come.

Nine days later I had an episode I thought was vertigo and unexpectedly had to be picked up by my husband and son. One week later I was in the emergency room slumped over to the left in a wheelchair with symptoms that appeared to be a stroke, or a brain tumor. How do you go from "I just got my dream" to "I don't know how my life will play out" in just nine days?

Overnight, the worst diagnoses were dismissed, but no answers surfaced. Curled up, lying on my left side to slow the spinning, I decided to shift to gratitude for my life *even if* it didn't look like it used to. I was released from the hospital with a vestibular migraine. Maybe. No further medical next steps were outlined because there were no real answers. Except I couldn't sit up, stand up, or walk.

We reached out to people who we knew were rooted in faith, asking for and receiving prayers from everywhere. I stacked up specialist appointments to continue looking for answers. I decided to ask for a thirty-day leave of absence. At that moment, I clearly knew I had to let go and choose my health over *all* else.

Dream careers, financial Excel documents, and budgets all fell off my radar. I focused on sitting upright in a rocker without falling over to the left, walking without a walker or furniture surfing, being thankful for our family and friends who surrounded us, cared for, and fed us for weeks.

I've never been able to sit more than a few minutes. Now I sat in the quiet, still house and didn't notice it had been hours. My brain was tired and needed complete and total rest. I had physical therapy, vision therapy, neurologists, and chiropractic care. I continued to improve daily by resting, sitting, and being grateful. My intention during this time was to listen for my next step. I heard "I am here" and "rest in me." So, I did. When I started to feel better, I was concerned the next words I heard would be "quit your job." Day by day I slowly regained balance and strength and returned cautiously to the office.

What I experienced once I was fully back to work was an *unexpected cultural shift*. My team members had stepped up to protect me from all stress during my rehabilitation. This example of supporting my health has become part of our new culture. We actively plan for and support our team members during vacation, maternity, and family crisis to ensure true respite and healing for our team. Our human bodies and brains are not designed for 24/7 activity.

In no way am I claiming I created a company shift this drastic by capturing my ideal scenario on a piece of trace paper. I am, however, genuinely grateful as I view my life through a lens that includes power, confidence, health, and always the choice to shift with intention.

Jennifer Graham graduated from Southern Illinois University Carbondale with a BS in Interior Design. She has thirty-five years of experience in corporate interior design, working with architectural firms, corporate furniture manufacturers, and dealerships. For seventeen years, she has been VP of Client Engagement + Workplace for Color-Art in St. Louis, Missouri. Color-Art assists corporate, education, and healthcare organizations realize and support their business objectives through the utilization of one of their most expensive assets, their space. Jennifer consults with clients to tie their culture, brand, and employee engagement into a space that allows innovation, connectivity, and trust, which leads to collaboration, efficiency, and market innovation. Jennifer's thirty-year marriage to Michael and their three independent, family-centric adult children are her greatest accomplishments. Jennifer and Mike share their authentic marriage, their time, and their mentorship as a model of the possibilities that can be created by building strong families and long-term committed relationships.

jgraham@color-art.com
www.linkedin.com/in/jennifergraham4525/
jennifergraham4525@gmail.com

TABETHA SHEAVER

Finding Your Fit

$25,000. That's what my life is worth. $25,000.

That is the underlying belief from which my other beliefs stem. All of them, even the good ones. I'll start by acknowledging I am an incredibly motivated, hardworking, driven, conscientious individual. To a fault. If I say I will do something, I do it. I respond this way because when I was six, seven, eight years old, I was told by my real dad he'd pick me up, and then he'd renege.

About this same time, my mom was getting remarried. The new man in our life wanted us to be a family. He wanted to adopt me. He sat me on the kitchen counter and asked me if I'd like that. We could be a family. We would go to Disneyland to celebrate.

I don't know how I knew, but I did. Part of the deal of adopting me was that my real dad's past-due child support of $25,000 would be forgiven in exchange for giving up his parental rights. Back then it seemed like a win-win.

Years later, I could see how my little brain would wire that arrangement into the beliefs that "If your own dad won't love you, how can anyone else?" and "Maybe if you can make more than $25,000, the world will know what you're worth."

After I was making more than five times the $25,000 mark, I still didn't feel worthy. By then, the patterns and behaviors were so entrenched, I just kept striving to prove myself. I took on anything. There wasn't anything that I couldn't figure out or accomplish.

I started leading teams, got my Project Management certification, then Change Management certification, and finally a Mediation certification. I built multiple businesses with people. I continued to "up" my game, but it was never enough.

Every day I would wake up with a small, nagging voice in my head that said, "Go to church." I had been to church a bit as a child, but I wasn't raised in any spiritual or religious context. I certainly had very little understanding of God or the Bible, much less big philosophical concepts like creation and purpose. I had a two-year-old, was seven months pregnant with my second child, had a new house, and was living the American dream. I wore busyness as a badge of honor. There was no way I had time to go to church, yet the voice continued. I finally Google-searched churches near me and acquiesced to the small, yet very persistent, voice in my head. Following that calling would be the first step in a transformation that would change my life and my family's life forever.

I have a great family. I'm "wanted." But outside my loving family unit, I never understood what it meant to be part of something bigger than yourself.

That day, in that church, was the beginning of people pouring into me, not because they wanted anything but because of what had been done for them and how their lives had been transformed.

I got intentional about going weekly, even when my son screamed bloody murder in the Sunday school until they would have to get me out of church. I was intentional about reading the Bible, to get through the whole thing so I could say I had done it in a year. I was intentional about asking questions when I was in doubt or did not understand. This was the first time I approached a situation without results or outcomes in mind. I had no idea what it meant to be "called" to do something.

You see, I was trained as a project manager, which meant I chose to control my world by creating a plan and controlling everyone to make sure that plan was executed as outlined.

Around that same time, I got promoted to CEO at the tech company where I worked. I had no idea how to be a CEO, so I went to the church and asked, "Who in our congregation can help me?" The answer: no one. The church was small, and most people were nurses or teachers, with possibly one business owner in the whole group.

So I did what everyone does when they don't know the answer. I googled it and found C12. C12 is a Christian CEO networking group devoted to helping leaders build greater businesses for a greater purpose. I joined.

One of the things you do in C12 is a core business presentation. As I was giving mine, someone in the group called me out on my pride. Painful but true. I really was proud that I was so busy, important, special, making so much money. In that moment, I recognized that for all my success, my hurting little seven-year-old self hadn't healed. Why? Because I needed a loving father to take care of me. I didn't need to work harder or to do more to show everyone I was OK. I was not OK. I was crumbling inside.

I had climbed the ladder, made it to the top, but all I got out of it was exhaustion. Nothing was ever good enough, big enough. Nothing I would ever do could fill the void.

I had no idea what made *Tabetha* happy. I was a chameleon. I liked whatever others liked, especially if I wanted to make a sale. To stop this behavior, I had to do things that felt foreign to me, like stopping, resting, doing nothing, not putting appointments on my calendar, not saying yes to make other people happy. It was time to find out what "I" liked.

While in the CEO role, I read a book called *Traction: Get a Grip on Your Business*. It offered simple concepts and a process that took people into consideration. I used these concepts to lead my team and get results. In addition, my C12 presentation guided me to quit the CEO role. It also helped me realize I had been leaning my career ladder on the wrong building.

Also, God, in an audible voice, told me to step out in faith and create my own company, Plus Delta 314, which helps employees impacted by technology understand what is being asked of them so they can change and learn new processes.

I discovered I'm a natural at Entrepreneurial Operating Systems (EOS) and that I really like engaging with entrepreneurs and their teams. Entrepreneurs who are on fire and passionate about their crafts or their causes often have deficits when it comes to managing people. Likewise, those people find leadership's demands and expectations daunting. For every change project, I facilitated conversations that revealed rampant frustration because the leader wasn't clear, had too many ideas, or was going too fast. Lack of clarity and an absence of alignment was stifling the organization's growth, which resulted in frustrated employees and unfulfilled visions and dreams. Many of the employees said they felt like no matter what they did, it was never enough. Sound familiar?

I realized we, as leaders, had to get better at helping people understand who they are, what they are made for, and how to teach them to become aligned with another's vision. That is how change happens.

Now I live the EOS life: doing what I love, with people I love, being compensated well, making a difference while having time for other things, like my ducks! I discovered I like ducks. And chickens. I discovered joy.

$25,000. That's it. That is what it costs per year for a team to collaborate with me to figure out who they are, what they were made for, and how to get in alignment so they can find joy in their business. I am intentional about finding time for me to feel fulfilled. I fill my cup so I can serve others—not so I can get higher on the corporate ladder but so I can reach a hand down to pull people up the ladder, helping them become the best versions of themselves.

I couldn't do it without belonging to a group of Christians who believe in something bigger than themselves, who take the time to listen to their creator and follow those callings.

What about you? If you are trying to do something only to fill a void, it won't work. If you are trying to do something to please other people, you just end up tired. When you make the choice to become who you were always meant to be, you are transformed.

Transformation starts with a belief that gets translated into a vision that requires people's support and making a choice to act. You are always *at choice*. Happy changing.

Tabetha Sheaver's first entrepreneurial venture left her frustrated and burnt out. She knew there had to be a better way. She pursued a certification from PMI.org, which led to consulting entrepreneurial leadership teams on process and change management. She increased revenue tenfold for two businesses prior to starting her own consulting firm and co-founded a platform for owners positioning their businesses for an exit. Since then, Tabetha has helped more than fifteen businesses in multiple industries understand the importance of people, processes, and data to drive *from vision down to execution*. Helping entrepreneurial leadership teams to be open, honest, and healthy so they can get things done is key because as the leadership team goes, so goes the organization. She is passionate about driving positive change in the world and believes there is no better way to grow and impact leaders, families, and communities than through the marketplace. Tabetha can be reached at:

www.plusdelta.com

Rejection to Respect

*I'd been waking up at 3:21 a.m. for months now,
but this time was different. I was lying face down on the thick carpet
in my family room asking, "Why, God, why?"*

The next thing I know, I'm writing in my journal. Through tears, I see blurry letters, R E S P E C T, as if written by another person. I was having an out-of-body experience. RESPECT? No way can I respect her decision to end our twelve-year marriage. Not without a fight.

Let me take you back to the summer before this 3:21 wake-up moment. We were visiting my sister in Cary, Illinois, and her friend says, "Your brother and his family make me sick. I mean look at them, it's like Ken and Barbie with their three perfect kids."

It did seem like we had the picture-perfect life. I was an attorney, vice president at a bank, and I coached little league baseball. The kids loved going to church and youth group. My wife was an amazing stay-at-home mom. We lived the quintessential middle-class life.

Then one evening, everything changed. I was in my walk-in closet getting ready for bed. My wife was at the sink brushing her teeth. The water turned off. I remember seeing a dab of toothpaste in the corner of her mouth as she came out to tell me, "I want a divorce."

Four dreadful words. I felt as if an elephant had smashed me into the wall and was still leaning on me. I couldn't breathe. I wanted to fight, or run, all those instincts triggering at once, except I couldn't move. I heard myself whimper, "No, please no, can't we figure this out?"

That's what started the 3:21 a.m. auto alarm every day for months.

Divorce isn't instant. We went the traditional route of marriage counseling, but after a few sessions, she said it wasn't working for her. I kept seeing that counselor, plus a pastor from our church, going to a men's group, and seeing a professional therapist. I was reading books, listening to podcasts, watching videos, searching for any way I could save my marriage. Nothing was working.

OK, the marriage wasn't as perfect as it looked, but really, it wasn't that bad. I mean it was way better than most other marriages I know. I thought it was so much better than my parents' fifty-year marriage. It had to be salvageable. I mean, we never fought. I kept digging in the dark for solutions, then it hit me. I was the only one trying to save the marriage.

I couldn't save it. I failed. I couldn't save my children from the pain of the divorce. I couldn't save our family from the financial pain of the divorce. I couldn't save myself from the embarrassment of failing at the biggest commitment in my life. My marriage was over. I had failed as a husband, as a father, and as a man.

Then life really started to unravel. I lost my job at the bank, they foreclosed on the house that I fought for and kept through the divorce, ending upside down by over $200,000. I had to file for bankruptcy. I lost everything. I rented two rooms in a friend's house to share with my three children who I had 50 percent custody of. At least I had that, thank God. The only thing that kept me from ending my life at that time was knowing I'd see my kids in a few days. I thought about suicide more often than I care to admit. I just couldn't do that to them. I told that little voice telling me I was a failure, that I wasn't good enough, to be still.

Now, let's get back to the out-of-body experience and the RESPECT thing. I didn't want to believe it, but deep in my soul I knew I had to respect her for realizing our marriage wasn't epic and that we both deserved epic. I wish we could have worked on that together, but she had been fighting this fight long before I engaged. I just didn't see it. I was clueless, even to the obvious. When I saw it, I didn't want to believe it. And it wasn't just our relationship. I finally saw that lack of respect was a problem in marriages all over the world. Relationships are shattered with misunderstanding and disrespect. There had to be a solution. I had to figure out what I did wrong so I wouldn't repeat it.

The quest took me to Tony Robbins. I'm not sure why I signed up for the event. I remember the sales guy finishing his pitch, "Tony Robbins has worked with presidents, Oprah, and Nelson Mandela for more than thirty years, so maybe he has something for you."

At my first event, I thought the whole thing was an elaborate stage performance. If you've never been to one of his live events, it's like a rock concert with highly devoted, raving fans. I'm there, by myself, cynical as hell, watching people race through the doors for the open seating like they were going to see Elvis. Then the music, dancing, and yelling starts.

I'm thinking, "Come on, just give me the CliffsNotes for this damn thing. Give me the secret sauce, Big Guy." (He is a giant.) I even sought out the people he had interventions with at the event to prove they were actors planted in the crowd. They weren't. Then, just before the fire walk (walking on two-thousand-degree hot coals), I have another of my out-of-body experiences. I see Oprah at the event. She is perfectly visible, about twenty rows in front of me. She is dancing, jumping around, and screaming. I say to myself, "She's worth a couple of billion dollars and she's playing full out, there's no way he's paying her off. Why am I holding back? What the heck did I come here for anyway? I came here to learn and change things in my life."

I drank the Kool-Aid; I mean, I sucked it down hard! I was all in, jumping up and down for the next four nights! I opened up to the energy. I loved learning what made me tick. My life has never been the same since that long weekend in Los Angeles.

I'd like to tell you that it only took one event with Tony Robbins to get "it." I wish I could tell you that over the next ten events with Tony Robbins, I would get "it." But I'm pretty stubborn, and I had a lot of stuff to rewire in my head. So, I read more books, attended more seminars, listened to more podcasts, spent thousands of hours and more money than I care to admit on learning about what makes people do the things they do. It has been four years, and I'm still getting "it."

It was on the Buddha deck at the O&O Academy in India that the *shifts* of all my *shit* came together to change my life and legacy. This time I was up at

4:40 a.m. due to excitement and jet lag rather than fear and anxiety. If fact, I was in a beautiful state. It was just before sunrise, and I was sitting on the gorgeous Buddha deck doing my morning meditation on the ocean. I started weeping, first with tears of gratitude and then, for a moment, tears of shame. Here it was again, that RESPECT thing. I had grown and learned so much. I had taken control of my emotions, I had let go of all the hurt, all the guilt, all the shame, the failures. (Quick mental edit: there are no failures, only lessons learned.) Just as I became aware that RESPECT was still missing, I had an epiphany. My lack of respect for women started with a lack of respect for my mom.

Now, this was a major kick in the ass. I am a self-proclaimed mama's boy. I'm her favorite. I love her dearly.

So why this realization? Because I felt her less than picture-perfect relationship with my dad was something she should never have tolerated. Then I smiled, feeling total respect for my mom flowing through me. She tolerated all of it for me, for her family, her grandchildren and the generations to come. She built a legacy of tolerance and grace, which isn't surprising, as her name is Grace.

I stepped off the deck into the warm Indian Ocean and wept happy, grateful tears. As the sun rose, I smiled, feeling my revelation sink even deeper. *There is something to appreciate and respect about every person and every situation that I experience.*

Now I have ultimate respect for my mom, my former spouse, my current partner, and for myself. I can comfortably and confidently tell you that, every day, I find *freedom in respect,* and so can you.

Matt Orzech is a divorce recovery specialist. Uniquely qualified as a self-help addict, a real estate junkie, and a recovering divorce attorney, Matt is dedicated to changing individuals' lives after divorce and other life transitions. Using his formal education, traditional counseling, church groups, self-help books, seminars, coaching, and life experiences, Matt crafted a master coaching practice to help others thrive after they survive. As CEO and Master Coach for his business, *Freedom in Relationships*, he developed *The Treasure Map to your Heart's Desires: Mastering your Emotional Intelligence so you can have Emotional Freedom*, a guide to a legendary life and epic relationships. Matt teaches that the quality of your life is *all* about the quality of your relationships: your relationship with your work, money, children, family, friends, spirituality, significant other, ex-significant others, your health, and ultimately the most important relationship of all, the relationship with yourself.

www.freedominrelationships.com
www.linkedin.com/in/matt-orzech-6647016
www.facebook.com/freedominrelationshipscoaching

Days of Darkness

I awake to blood on my pillowcase.

I looked at the clock. I was going to be late for work, again. In my rush to get ready, I glanced into the bathroom mirror. My two front teeth were chipped, and my face was covered in blood. I didn't recognize the person staring back and, to this day, I have no memory of what caused the damage to my face.

Two years previously, my husband had left me because he was convinced I had been sleeping around. About that time, I suffered a miscarriage. From then on, the bottle consumed me. I turned away from music, love, my voice, and God.

While preparing for a divorce at the age of twenty-five, I bitterly quit my band. There were no words, no songs to sing in my heart. The life I thought I was going to have was wrecked. My heart was an empty void I desperately wanted to fill. I was young, naïve, inexperienced, lost, and alone.

I told my father about my ordeal, knowing he would provide support. He organized a trip to Serbia for me for a month. Seeing my roots and attending an incredible four-day festival called "Exit" gave me perspective on a new life. It showed me I could not give up on music. And I could finally accept that my ex-husband was never coming back. I realized it was time to look out for myself and figure out how to grow independently.

After I returned to the States, I went back to school to study music, during which I worked in retail. The divorce caused many of my friends from high school to leave. They believed my ex-husband's view of our private affairs. That meant I had little or no support as I reformed my life.

I studied and met new people, but my real pleasure was burying myself in books about romance and exciting worlds of intrigue. It started, oddly enough, with a three-book set that my ex-husband had given to me. That's when the devil and his underworld sought me out, and I strayed the path for several years before becoming who I am today.

In February 2011, one phone call with a friend from high school shifted me into the depths of the Chicago BDSM community. (BDSM is an acronym for "bondage, discipline (or domination), sadism, and masochism" as a type of sexual practice.) Now, many have an opinion or idea about the BDSM community or what "BDSM" means, but if you have not walked into a dungeon/underground bar and truly met the people in this community, then the knowledge you have is likely drawn from *Fifty Shades of Grey* or an online forum. In my curiosity to explore, I found an intriguing part of myself again, and wanted to uncover more of my sexuality.

Like any community, group, fraternity, or cult, there are positives and negatives. Entering into this underground world, I discovered all types of people, sexual orientations, dynamics, and professions. The parties, costumes, drinks, and late nights were all delightful until the "other shoe" dropped and I saw the other side. As I witnessed and experienced abuse, sexual assault, harassment, and humiliation, I entered into what felt like a karmic journey. I stepped out of my physical body and unearthed the awareness that I had been here before. Not just the concept of reincarnation but replaying old wounds, deliberately hurting myself, engaging in a cycle of people-pleasing self-sabotage. I relived pain–physically, emotionally, and spiritually.

My spirit was asleep and numb. I could feel my soul trying to claw its way out, but my shadow was gluttonous . . . a very hard sin. With so much trauma and pain, it is hard to stop and turn away from what is familiar, even if it is harmful. For several years, I was a hamster in a wheel, continually numbing myself with toxins: alcohol, fake friends, gossip, and an artificial sense of community. As lost as I was, I did meet a few angels among the energy vampires, demons, and dark energies. I still communicate with those angels, and, thanks to them, I am stronger for it.

Struggling in school and going nowhere, I took a songwriting class to get back to my passion, my dream. I met a talented bass player. Throughout our semester together, we'd have brief discussions on life, music, and philosophy. He was older, and I was one of the few in the class who took time to get to know him. I didn't know he'd been put on my path for a reason.

One evening I called him on the phone to discuss a project idea. We started talking about other things, and he asked me, "Do you accept Jesus Christ as your Lord and personal Savior?"

I do not know how or why the conversation led him to ask me such a question, but the moment is engrained in my memory because of the power of the exchange.

I paused, allowing my shadow-self to laugh at even talking about Jesus.

His question reminded me of talks with my mother in my high-school years, and how I dismissed her, rolling my eyes and calling her a Christian extremist.

I told him, "I haven't thought of God for several years." Then I explained my pain with my miscarriage and my ex-husband and acknowledged, "I no longer pray or even think about the light."

He then asked me, "Would you be willing to say it out loud?"

I was skeptical that saying this simple phrase would affect the hell I was experiencing, but I did agree, hesitantly.

He heard my underlying skepticism and suggested, "Let's say it together."

There were knots of fear in my chest and stomach. Part of me was defensive and resisted saying the words. But deep inside, beyond the ego and fear, my soul called out to say it. I took a deep breath and exhaled and said the acceptance of Jesus Christ in my life.

Before hanging up the phone, he stated he would pray for me. I began sobbing uncontrollably, my chest expanding and collapsing with each breath. I remember it all vividly and believe that by accepting God (and the light), my heart began to heal. It was my cry for forgiveness, love, and mercy. God heard me.

I began taking responsibility for my actions. I admitted to a former lover that I was, indeed, an alcoholic, that I knew I had to change, and that I needed his help. He agreed to be my sponsor. He applied his knowledge and experience both in social work and as an AA member to create a structure that led me to my sobriety. He is still my sponsor.

From that moment of evoking the light, God, Universe—however you wish to define or label this loving energy—it has drawn me as a beacon to other healers. I have realized the accumulative effort of major spiritual cleansing and healing. Like a sponge, I absorbed all teachings and focused on my spiritual development. I wanted to find inner peace and hold onto this connection. I tried crystal healing, past-life hypnosis, energy and aura cleansing by two healers. I read all kinds of metaphysical books, listened to lectures and speakers in the spiritual development arena. I began to understand the teachings of manifestation, cause and effect, chakra healing, my natal chart in astrology, and shadow work.

After the cleansing by the two healers, they advised me to not expose myself to certain environments anymore, to let go of those around me who did not serve my highest good, and to protect, love, and value my energy in this vessel.

Since 2014, my life has opened up to so many gifts. I have come to accept my emotional self by reflecting on the years when it was common for me to internalize my pain, allow my ego to run free and judge, fear, envy, hate, and manipulate those around me, cleverly affirming the saying that "misery loves company."

Once I put the proper tools into practice and dedicated myself, God (the light) was shown to me in many forms: pennies on the street, feathers in the air or ground, birds passing, angel numbers in sequences of 111, 222, 333, 444, and 555. Messages and wisdom through people, places, and things were presented to me, revealing "the light" that was intended for me, to help me keep my faith and stay grounded.

I have been sober eight years. All of the spiritual practices I opened up to truly saved me from alcoholism. Alongside my personal soul work, I apply these same insights and practices with my present clients. My transformation led me to constantly put good intentions into my actions, needs, and desires. My motto is "it's simple, but it isn't easy." Achieving grace requires courageous commitment every single day.

Fedra Ekres is a singer, songwriter, and healer. Born in Novi Sad, Serbia, and raised in Chicago, her journey into music started after remission from children's leukemia at the age of five. She would sing everything from cartoons to jazz music during chemotherapy. In high school, with influence from her mother's side of the family, she studied tarot, mysticism, and crystal-healing. During the pandemic lockdowns, she became a Reiki master healer. Currently residing in Bradenton, Florida, she is following both her musical profession and that of a Reiki master healer. She released her solo album, *Fedra, I AM*, and is working on her first single, "See the Light." She views performing on stage as the fullest expression of herself, and believes that by creating an affirming vocal message, people on Earth can join together in harmony to effect sustainable change, starting with our home.

www.fedraekres.com
fedraekres@gmail.com
www.instagram.com/fedraekres
www.facebook.com/fedra.ekres

JAYME KNIGHT

The Phone Call

I think I'm getting let go.

I never imagined I would be saying these words to my family, especially not Monday morning after Christmas 2020. As I waited for the dreaded phone call, I tried to hold back tears. How could this happen? I was sad, nervous, scared, and uncertain about what was to come. I poured my heart and soul into everything I did.

My three kiddos were home on winter break, and I was hoping they wouldn't notice the change in my demeanor. At that moment, they noticed and quickly whispered, "We love you, Mommy." With those precious words, I knew it was God's way of saying, "You are not alone."

The Ever-Changing Calling

I've always wanted to be a teacher, but I kept changing my mind about which subject to teach. One day I realized physical education was my calling!

Growing up, I always played sports. But after high school graduation, that changed. "Recreational play" was all I saw in college. There were no practices, except lifting a drink to my mouth during games!

With inactivity and not the best diet, the dreaded freshman fifteen was real. This was new to me. I always "trained" for the game. When I removed practices and games from my daily routine, I didn't have a backup plan to keep my mind and body healthy.

Renewed Purpose—Help Youth Stay Healthy

After the weight gain, I realized I needed to educate the younger generation on the importance of training not for "the game" but for their personal health! I thought fitness and teaching were my forever career.

Plans Change—Finances Strained

Fast-forward years later to marriage and one kid. When Tucker, my firstborn, entered this world, I wanted to be a stay-at-home mom. When my husband left for work at 5:30 a.m., I called him crying because I didn't want to go back to work. I loved teaching, and yet being a mom had become everything to me.

Unfortunately, we were not in a financial position for me to stay at home. With the addition of McKinley and Ryder, that changed. The cost of childcare did not add up to my take-home pay. I decided to stay home. I was in heaven! However, my husband was less than thrilled that I gave up my teaching career with benefits and a great retirement plan.

Strain and Gain

Was it a strain on my marriage and our finances? You betcha! However, I was determined to make it work because I wanted to be the one taking pictures and sending them to friends and family, not missing events and receiving texts and images from others. I wanted to live my motto:

"We have one life to live, so do what makes you happy."

Help From Social Media

I loved my kids and being with them, but I also needed something for me. One day, a social media ad popped up telling me to join an exercise boot camp for *free*. God's divine intervention was at work! Little did I know the true impact this boot camp community would have on me.

God knew I needed these free thirty days at that point in my life! Plus, I wouldn't have to feel guilty about spending money on myself.

A Month of Rejuvenation

In those thirty days, I found a community that inspired, supported, and motivated me. But I knew I could not afford a membership. While it was worth every penny, it wasn't something we could add to our budget.

God, please help me find a way!

In an effort to add value, I followed the owner and head trainer on social media and offered words of encouragement.

An Exciting Invitation

My persistence and enthusiasm paid off! I began subbing occasionally in child watch and at the front desk. I found myself helping more and more. Being there made me feel good on the inside, and my kids loved it too!

Then, the phone call I had been waiting for: "We're ready to add kids camp to the schedule. Would you like to be the trainer?"

"Yes!" My heart was exploding.

My passion for helping others was recognized and opened more opportunities in the gym. God was at work! The path he chose was being laid out before me. Or so I thought. I wore several hats and helped open three more gyms before I received "the dreaded phone call."

The Pandemic Changed Everything

None of us were prepared for a pandemic that shut down everything. We all wondered how to navigate this unknown. I knew for sure that this gym was needed. Our doors must remain open.

God heard numerous prayers during all this "crazy."

When members continued to pay top dollar, with doors temporarily closed and only Zoom workouts or replays keeping people active, I knew God was providing.

The members of this community showed up repeatedly for the gym and each other. The countless acts of kindness were nonstop, and I was once again reminded of why I belonged here. God opened the door to a whole new world for me when that gym promotion came across my social media feed. I was sure I'd finally found my purpose, but I was wrong!

Change of Life Plans

God knew it was only temporary. I did not! He had different plans for me. I remember it vividly. My phone rang, and the owner asked if I had our meeting on my schedule. I did, but was asked to do it in person.

My response was, "Are you firing me because of something I did, or laying me off because of the pandemic?"

In that moment in time, everything changed. To be let go from the one place where I felt special was devastating. Now what? What would I do next? I felt this huge void. I was afraid of the unknown and leaving everything I'd worked so hard to achieve.

Trust God and Lean In

After hanging up from "the phone call," I prayed and leaned into God. My trust in him was at an all-time high. It had to be. If I didn't have him, I would have been lost. I dug deep into my faith and continued to ask God for his strength, love, and support. Daily I kept asking him:

What's my purpose? What are your plans for me?

Then one day, I got another life-changing phone call that resulted in yet another career switch—from fitness to finance!

Another Change at My Age?

Really? At forty-four years old, the thought of starting over was daunting. Would I succeed or fail? As soon as I thought of failing again, it occurred to me that I hadn't failed at anything. I'd been successful with each career and commitment I'd made.

The world changes. Life changes. Without being aware, I'd been bravely changing all along the way. This switch was also about helping people, just as I'd been doing, only from a different approach.

I recognized my overarching purpose was helping others reach their goals, find happiness, and accomplish something they didn't think was possible. That realization filled me with joy!

Mortgage Lending? Really? I'm All In!

After a single conversation with one of the owners of Homestead Financial Mortgage, I knew this was the right change. I had an overwhelming feeling of calm and peace. I took the leap of faith and went all in. Again!

This new career and Homestead were for me! I passed my Residential Mortgage Loan Advisor exam and began working as a loan advisor.

When I think back to the "dreaded phone call," I understand why it happened. It was *not* my plan, but his. To fulfill my purpose, to be successful, happy, and ready to make a more significant impact on this world, one door had to close so another could open. Normally, I would have begged for that door to reopen, but instead I chose to trust God and let him take the lead.

Finally, Work-Life Balance

Although my kids are older, I'll always be there for them when they need me. Now I love being able to support both my family and our financial goals. Being a loan advisor fulfills both my desire to balance my life and to help others.

A Company with Value and Integrity

I am blessed to work for a company that values its clients and employees and always looks out for their best interests. When someone asks what I do, I beam. I love getting to know my clients, learning about their needs, and finding ways to help them!

What Have I Learned?

Never be afraid of "the phone call." It may lead to greater happiness and more adventures. Be fearless in trying that next new thing. People have multiple careers these days. Jobs are changing all the time in response to new demands and restrictions. When one door closes, lean in and be ready for that next door to open! Trust God's plan!

Jayme Knight, a native of Saint Louis, Missouri, graduated (years ago) with a BS in Education and went on to earn her master's from Lindenwood University. Although she had a background in teaching and fitness, she found her true purpose as a Mortgage Loan Advisor in her forties. That career move combined her teaching skills with her desire to help others. Jayme values the connections she makes with her clients. She enjoys getting to know them and supporting them on the roller coaster ride of homeownership! Her positive attitude and enthusiastic support help her clients and business partners succeed. Jayme works tirelessly to help those she serves, which is evident on her social media channels and podcasts. Jayme enjoys making memories with family and friends, her gym time, and loving her kiddos: Tucker, McKinley, and Ryder! Her prayer is to make them proud, even when she fails!

www.facebook.com/jaymeknightlo
www.linkedin.com/in/jayme-knight-lo

JOHN H. RIELLY

The Whistler Adventure

Face of God

In late 2018, I was invited to attend a financial seminar hosted by Tony Robbins in Whistler, British Columbia, Canada. My original plan was to fly into Vancouver for a couple of days and then take a shuttle to Whistler. A late-breaking snowstorm was predicted for the Midwestern United States, so I flew out to Vancouver a day early. There were about one-hundred friends in the hotel, and a wonderful time was had by all.

Tony Robbins has a small group, which I joined in Chicago in 2018. I met a woman and we agreed to spend time together before the seminar began. She had left for Whistler, and she invited me to join her there. The shuttle was not leaving for several days, so I hired a driver to pick me up that day. My friend expressed interest in going on a dogsled trip, and she started reaching out to the providers to set up our outing. Unfortunately, I was not able to get to Whistler in time to go dogsledding that day. We met in the lobby of the hotel where the conference was being held. We decided to go on a snowmobiling trip the following day. The outfitter required that we sign waivers, pay for liability insurance, and wear a helmet. Ordinarily, I would have refused all!

The morning dawned brilliantly over Whistler. My friend and I met at the coffee shop and grabbed some caffeinated beverages. A shuttle picked us up and we headed out. I had been snowmobiling before, but she was more of a newcomer. We had our own sleds, and I followed her. We rode to a cabin in the wilderness where our advance team prepared us a wonderful breakfast. The combination of additional caffeine and my inability to zoom across the snow was becoming a great challenge. We set out for the lodge. I would stop for a while, let the group get ahead of me, then I would drive my machine more quickly to catch up. The group crossed a fifty-foot-wide cleared path and waited for the others to catch up. I took that opportunity to open the throttle completely and speed across the snow!

The next thing I remember was hearing crashing metal, flying downhill, and smashing into a tree that stopped my descent. I knew I was in a bad place, but I instinctively knew my neck wasn't damaged. The mountain guide who had been leading us quickly came to my side. I told him I couldn't breathe. He helped me out of the tree and lay me down in a stone-covered streambed. I could see the snowmobile, which had dived into the ground and was pointing up into the sky.

After the guide knew I was safe, he left to organize my rescue. That is when I knew I was in real trouble. I had dressed in layers of waterproof clothing, so I was warm, dry, and flat on my back. I knew my body was badly broken, but the shock of the accident kept the pain at bay. I noticed that one of the trees had a leaf remaining on it. I saw it as the face of God that so many people have described. I prayed silently for God to please deliver me into the best possible place that there could be. I was born into a Roman Catholic family, and I was a practicing member of the church. But despite decades of praying, I could not remember any of the prayers of my youth, so I had a personal conversation with God.

A group of guides ministered to my health. Trained years ago as a ski patrol guide and having advanced training from the American Red Cross, I could tell by their questions that I was in good hands. They attached me to a backboard and lifted me to the surface. I don't know how long the process took, but it was an ordeal. When we reached the main road, I was attached to a snowmobile and then towed to a mountain lodge clinic where the doctors decided my injuries were serious enough to require an immediate transfer to Vancouver. I was reattached to the snowmobile and taken to an ambulance that took me to the helipad. The medics wouldn't give me any narcotics and the pain was really setting in. I heard the rotors of the helicopter, felt the prick of the needle—then sleep.

When I woke up, I was informed I'd had surgery for my crushed pelvis, nine rib fractures, and a lacerated spleen. I'd required three pints of blood, had blood on my brain, and two nicked vertebrae. I had a chest tube to drain the blood from my lungs, heart monitors, oxygen, and IVs (though I still ended up with pneumonia).

I was in a dark mental place as I learned what I had been through and what was in store in the weeks and months to come. Vancouver is 2,552 miles from my home in Columbus, Ohio. I felt so alone. I remembered there was a bottle of prescribed sleeping medicine in my hotel room, so I asked if I could be "temporarily" released from the hospital. I'd go back to the hotel, take a shower, have some food and come back. My real thought was to grab that medication, take all the sleeping pills, and check out from the pain I was experiencing and from what was ahead.

What I did not know was that the Tony Robbins family was working for me behind the scenes. I had texted some of the staff, and they had gotten the word out. My good friend Misti Wriston (who has her story on some of the other pages of this book) responded massively! Several of the attendees at the event in Whistler made their way nearly eighty miles to visit me in the hospital. Friends sent and brought flowers, balloons, Diet Cokes, and beverages from Starbucks. People I barely knew—some complete strangers—were emailing, texting, calling, and, most importantly, praying for me! My dear friend Ruth Hiller arranged a fundraiser that paid for a four-day visit from my two daughters, Michele and Alison.

I grew up in a Roman Catholic family with a belief in the Christian God. My relationship was along the lines of seeing God as someone to respect. My experience lying on that frozen creek bed with a five-hundred-pound snowmobile towering over me, knowing I was badly injured and completely powerless, was strangely enlightening. God's face that I'd seen in the leaf was friendly and loving. As terrifying as the situation was, I felt warm and loved.

Misti encouraged me to reach out to everyone and allow the generosity that people were offering to wash over me. I resisted the love and support for a while. I really didn't feel worthy of receiving that love. I hallucinated that I would "owe" people, that I could never repay them for their generosity. I finally did make that shift, and the outpouring of messages and prayers confirmed to me that there is an ever-loving God. Whenever I am tempted to revert to my old ways, I simply have to login to Facebook or WhatsApp and see that there are people constantly helping others for no other reason than it is the right thing to do! Scott Humphrey is the leader of the Tony Robbins group, Platinum Partners, of which I am a member. He and his wife, Corrine, came to the hospital several times. On one of their visits, they brought me a laptop. Tony even dropped by with his security staff, who each wished me well.

The day-to-day in the hospital was a grind despite the love surrounding me. I couldn't get out of bed except when I was getting a scan. One day, two staff members entered and announced that they were with the "physio department." That is physical therapy for us in the next country to the south of Canada. They announced that I was going to stand up! I remember thinking they were crazy. But after hearing the voices of encouragement from all my amazing supporters, I agreed to give it a try. After moving the trays and machines I was connected to, they supported me, eventually getting me on my feet!

My insurance company finally arranged for my return to Ohio. I was admitted to a hospital in Columbus and then transferred to a rehabilitation center where my progress continued. Now, more than three years later, I still feel the metal in my body from the surgeries. But more significantly than that is the love I hold in my heart—love for the amazing and generous people who came to my aid in my time of need, and a new, profound love of God! I am committed to living a more generous and grateful life. I am blessed!

John H. Rielly was born and raised in Cincinnati, Ohio. He graduated from Xavier University and has an MBA. He is a proud father of two beautiful and talented daughters, Michele and Alison Rielly

MEGAN DIRKS

Breaking. Melting. Changing.

This is a story about how a hike in my favorite national park depicts my journey home to myself.

Grinnell Glacier is an 11.2 mile out-and-back trail in Glacier National Park. Once past Swiftcurrent Lake and Lake Josephine, I started to gain some elevation and views of Grinnell Lake. Glaciers started to dominate the backdrop as I continued to climb, the elevation making catching my breath time well spent. Eventually, I came to Grinnell itself, where I was drawn down to Upper Grinnell Lake.

I spent an afternoon here, inches from the glacial waters created by the melt off from the glacier itself. Lying there, I closed my eyes and listened to the stillness, allowing the calm to envelope me. I repeatedly heard sounds reminiscent of thunder as the packed snow and ice cracked under the heat of the sun, a beautiful and painful sound. Natural and raw. Heavy with a reminder that *she's breaking and melting, changing.*

How I got there that day is simple. I drove to the trailhead, hiked for six hours, and came out equally energized and exhausted. How I ended up on a hike in my twenty-second national park of the year is a bit more involved. How I got to a point where the glaciers of my own life started melting for the better is why I am writing this chapter of my life.

By definition, a glacier is described as a persistent body of dense ice that is constantly moving under its own weight. Like a glacier, I have spent much of my life moving under what I thought was my own weight. And of course, some of that weight is mine to hold. But a lot of weight had been piled on by others, society, and my own need to control, to do more, or to accommodate others. It got heavy.

This came to a head as I rolled into my thirtieth year of life with my tank on empty. I was successful, in a loving relationship, had wonderful friends, support-ive family, and several degrees under my belt. I had traveled the world, competed in bodybuilding, modeled, sat on a board, and was a few years into my aerial acrobatics career. *But I was tired.*

Unexplainable health issues were controlling my life. I was constantly bloated, without energy, had brain fog, and was simply not myself. Doctors either couldn't help me or treated me like I was making everything up. When I wasn't working or sleeping, I acted as my own advocate, researching my issues, changing my life-style, and obsessing over my health. Restrictions became my closest companion.

Underneath the physical manifestations, I also had a nagging feeling that I was lost. That my compass was somehow off. That I didn't know who I was or who I wanted to be. It created issues in my relationship, which ended, landing me on an important path to finding myself.

I would spend the next two years navigating the beginning of my journey inward, supported by a wonderful team of doctors and good humans at Palm Health in St. Louis. There, I was taught to see myself as a mind, body, and soul, and I got answers to my multiple health and autoimmune conditions.

I started to recognize that my jam-packed schedule and always-busy-to-a-fault lifestyle were unhealthy ways of distracting myself from things I didn't want to face. Slowing down and doing the work to identify patterns allowed me to see that, for years, I'd morphed into what I thought others wanted of me. I conformed to fit in. I was saying yes to all the wrong things. I came to understand Gabor Mate's belief that if you can't say no, your body will do it for you.

It would take my therapist asking me if I was safe in my newest "situation-ship" for me to finally admit how much I'd contorted myself to be with a guy, even if that meant putting up with manipulation, abuse, or toxic behavior. I took whatever came along. At thirty-two, I made an intentional and necessary choice to be single. No more dating. I decided with clarity and conviction that I was willing to sit in whatever feelings would come from not having a distraction or a safety blanket, and that I would do so for as long as it took for me understand my own power.

It was at this time that I started to lean into intention-setting, which is how I came to create my *2020 intention of being better at being alone*. I wanted to get to a point where I didn't feel lonely without a partner. I wanted to learn to be more comfortable in my own company, rather than depending on the availability of friends or a partner to do something with me. While I had lived alone for years and was generally independent, I was caught in the habit of needing someone or something outside myself to affirm *I was enough*.

Did I manifest the global pandemic that forced many of us to be alone more than we were used to? I sure hope not. But, for me personally, it provided so many opportunities to learn, grow, and recalibrate.

This energy continued into 2021 with a new strength, supported by a new intention: *living with authenticity*. Now that I was comfortable in my own company, I wanted to focus on being more of my authentic self, to gain a clearer understanding of who that was, and to *embody her*. I wanted to learn to trust my intuition. I wanted to *be me, unapologetically*.

After setting this intention, I had a powerful yearning to get in the car and go. Where? I didn't know. To do what? Also didn't know. But it all fell into place as opportunities to travel and explore gravitated to me. I spent the majority of 2021 on the road, mostly alone. I drove over 13,000 miles, across twenty-four states, mostly alone. I hiked countless trails within twenty-five national parks, mostly alone. The time I spent in my own company, with only my thoughts and the open road, were hours I would have never been able to bear until then. The time spent in the great outdoors without connection to cell service and away from civilization and other humans became my favorite pastime. Much of this I did without a solid plan, scheduled spontaneously. I started to let go of expectations and restrictions I'd accepted. I found balance, let go of some of my Type A tendencies, and learned to trust what was presented to me.

Concurrently, I spent a significant chunk of time chipping away at layers of myself that weren't who I really was or wanted to be: the parts I silenced, shied away from, and, in some ways, was ashamed of. This was due in large part to switching to EMDR therapy early in the year, which helped me understand how much of myself had been buried under various forms of trauma. I could write volumes about how life-changing this has been, how I processed more in a year with this therapist than I did in eighteen years of combined therapy. But that experience deserves its own story.

For now, know that for the first time in my adult life, I felt light. I believed, without a shadow of a doubt, that I was on the right path. I felt connected to me, a feeling that has drawn people, opportunities, and experiences to me like a magnet. In many cases, that's been a good thing. In others, they've been brought to me to learn a lesson, to test my still-maturing love of self, or to practice protecting my peace. Most significantly, I found my voice. The authentic me who I hid underneath expectations, people-pleasing, fear of being hurt, and trauma responses finally took center stage. I began to write again. I learned to stand up for myself in situations where I would have previously silenced myself. I was actively giving myself permission to be who my soul knew me to be.

What you'll see of my life now is me finally moving under my own weight, embodying those Grinnell Glacier vibes after melting off some of the burden of others' opinions or restrictions on me. I released my own need to control, achieve, or have a plan. I no longer wait for someone to do things with. Those dense parts of my life are melting, breaking, and disappearing. They're not gone, and there's still more to learn, but this new weightlessness has allowed me to use my voice, set better boundaries, ignore certain societal pressures, and go with the flow. I have stopped depending on others in areas where I can now depend on myself.

I have found me.

Megan Dirks is a former teacher turned IT consultant. When she isn't traveling, she fosters animals, coaches, and practices the aerial arts, is an avid reader, and can often be found writing in a local coffee shop. She earned an undergraduate degree in Business Administration and a minor in Leadership Studies from Kansas State University, and is also a dual degree master's graduate, obtaining a Master of Business Administration and a Master of Educational Leadership from Saint Louis University. Megan is a certified well-being coach through the Anthropedia Foundation. Her experience as a Teach For America corps member validated her passion for impacting others through teaching, guiding, and sharing experiences. At the time of this writing, Megan flexes that muscle through sharing her travel experiences, learnings from her loss of health, and her mental health journey.

www.linkedin.com/in/megan-dirks-8a958912/

The Formula

Be Who You Want To Be

In my youth, I was an introvert. Like most introverts, it wasn't that I didn't like people, it was that I just didn't understand people. You get it. And perhaps, like me, you know there's more you can do. Wanting to know and become more guided me to my purpose and life's work. I also gained wisdom, not just about myself, but about you. That's why my chapter is in this anthology. To help you apply the formula to benefit your life. Here's the story.

I started a company in 2003 with my best friend since the first grade, Nick, and we hired consultants to help with that business. One consultant we hired, Grant, was an expert at using assessment tools to help others. Little did I know, this relationship would change the trajectory of my life. Now, I pass it on to you.

I first used the assessment tools to gain a better understanding of myself. Then, I applied what I learned to help me understand other people. Understanding the differences between people made me a better communicator—in business, as a manager, as a father, as a friend.

One of the most applicable things I discovered was that there are certain parts of us that assessments can measure, but which are very, very difficult to change. Likewise, there are other parts of us which we can assess and are easier to change.

When I sold my past business with Nick and founded a consulting company, I knew that the best way to grow a business was through referrals and networking. If you are an introvert, you know those things are NOT our cup of tea! I used the assessment tools as a map to develop more skills around the things that

I needed, like interpersonal skills, understanding others, diplomacy and tact. I built those skills and "*bolted* them onto my personality." Personalities are among the things that are not easy to change; however, skills can be developed. So, I, an introvert who wasn't comfortable networking, taught myself to be a skilled networking extrovert.

The first two presentations I gave to groups were scary! The crowd was straight-faced, arms-crossed, seemingly uninterested. I was nervous. I was afraid I was disappointing the host. I didn't know if I was delivering the message they came for. The next day my inbox was full. Those folks were contemplating what I shared, and the next day reached out for my help. They were not judging the presentation.

Ok. Now what? To get better, I needed practice. I called my friend, Elizabeth for her Dale Carnegie training on presentations, and I am 300% better for having done it.

I never felt skilled at quickly thinking on my feet. So, I asked someone, "how do you learn how to think and speak in the heat of the moment?" After some thought, they said "find an improv class." Are you kidding me? Definitely not my style! Speaking on stage with a group making up stories you must play along with? It was eight weeks of the most terrifying, horrible training (for my style), yet one of the best learning experiences of my life.

I learned I could do the hard thing, that it's worth it. You can, too.

Then, I had a conversation with myself that led to an inspiring thought. "Art, you've been studying and practicing the models for who you could become, IF you wanted to change anything about yourself. So, who DO YOU want to become?"

This conversation provoked another scary decision which caused me to remind myself, that with time and practice, everything becomes easier. Imagine an "introvert" having an international business on six continents, giving presentations to groups of 400+ people, selling services to strangers, developing fun relationships which turn into the richest friendship. That's what I have learned.

YOU can, too.

Whether you identify as an introvert or an extrovert, you probably have a few things you'd like to adjust about yourself. You can. There's an easy formula, and I'm delighted to share it with you.

1. Self-Awareness – KNOW Yourself
2. Self-Development – GROW Yourself
3. Self-Display – SHOW Yourself

Knowing yourself is the first step. Your personal skills, personality style, preferences, values, passions and how you think about things is the perfect place to start. Understanding these things is the jumping off point for self-acceptance and the beginning of your journey, if you choose.

Growing yourself IS the journey (if you choose). See the gaps between who you are and who you want to be. Focus on the gaps and look for resources that can help you improve, like books, videos, friends, consultants, coaches. Whatever it takes. Then practice. These skills are like muscles. We have to go to the "gym" to make them grow. Ok, don't go to the gym. You get it. Practice is key.

Showing yourself is about giving yourself to the world. You are an amazing, unique, never-seen-before, wonderful person! There are people who love you. You may not know it yet, but there are people *who need you*. It could be four people or four thousand people… that isn't important. You are here to make ripples and touch others' lives. You already have. You're going to do it more. Show yourself to others. Give yourself to others. It will come back to you in so many rewarding ways. I promise. I hope this chapter inspires you to:

KNOW. GROW. SHOW.

Art Snarzyk is known as "The Turnover Terminator" for his unique way of helping business owners and managers select and manage only ideal, top-performing staff. *The Small Business Monthly* named him one of the "Top 100 St. Louisans You Should Know To Succeed In Business." His consulting company, InnerView Advisors works with contractors and professional service businesses worldwide to become better at attracting, hiring, and retaining great employees who fit their unique companies.

www.InnerViewAdvisors.com

Just a Girl (from the Shadows) Basking In My Light

Sitting in my prayer chair, wondering what I will write.

I pray about what to share with you, what story to tell about the shifts that have brought me to this moment, writing my story for you!

It's an awkward prayer, wondering what to share with the world, wanting to inspire others that their shift is possible too, all within a limited number of words; but I prayed, and I listened. I reminisced about the many shifts that have happened throughout my life, observing the silver thread that weaves throughout, connecting all the God-whispers, the kairos[1] moments, the divine interruptions that have shifted my life and aligned me with my purpose!

I have an image of myself as a child, being hurt. Every time I got excited about something and wanted to be noticed, I got hurt. I loved gymnastics! When I was eight, I would get dropped off at the YMCA for swimming and gymnastics lessons. I would skip swimming, because swimming was scary. I would wander around the Y for an hour, waiting for gymnastics to start. On the day my parents were supposed to come to the Y and see what I had learned, I had to tell them I had skipped swimming classes. My dad was furious and told me I couldn't do gymnastics anymore. That hurt!

When I was ten, I wanted to show off for my mom and brother and tried to leap over a metal kitchen chair with pointy corners. As I made this great leap, my inner thighs caught the two pointy parts. The chair and I both toppled. I ended

179

up with huge bruises on my legs, and my confidence was also bruised! While there were many incidents, these two were just part of the programming that taught me doing something exciting hurts. I learned to play it safe, to stay in the background, to hide and not cause trouble. All of this was programmed into me before I was even a teenager!

The programming we take in as children is crazy powerful! I stayed in the background, hid in my shadows, and stayed out of trouble for most of my young life. I was on the soccer team in elementary school for a few weeks, but when my family showed no interest in me being on the team, I quit. Why try to be seen? I didn't sign up for art classes, I didn't get a job in high school, I didn't go to parties, I didn't drink; I hid, and I watched everyone else live life. I didn't want to get hurt or in trouble. I became invisible. I was programmed.

My programming continued into my adult life. At twenty-one, I married the first boy I dated because I thought no one else would ever see me in my shadows. I left after four years. That was my first conscious shift, the first time I chose to see myself. This began a series of shifts that have brought me to here, now!

Have you ever felt like this? Have you ever hidden and felt completely invisible? Have you ever known that you can't figure out how to fully be you? It's hard to overcome that programming! It gets so deeply woven into us! At the same time, it feels like it can all unravel and fall apart. You know what I mean . . . don't you?

As I sat in that prayer chair praying about what to share, I wondered how I got from there to here. How did I go from hiding out in my shadows to basking in my light? How did I go from staying out of trouble to living with adventure and joy? (I still don't make a lot of trouble, but I do have a lot more fun!) How did life shift for me?

I define *shift* as releasing the old stuff—the hurts and the programming—and then creating space and awareness to be open to receive. "Receive what?" you ask. The signs and messages that my intuition was now allowing in, guiding me into my journey and my purpose.

How did I shift? Gratitude. Simple, yet profound! Gratitude puts me in a place of being so thankful for everything in my life: the great, the good, the mundane, even the struggles.

If I allow myself to sink back into my shadows, I go down hard, and it gets me *nowhere*!

However, if I choose to be grateful for everything, something amazing happens:

- I have a migraine headache, and I get the rest my body desires.
- The bank takes forever to close on our loan, and we get the blessings of better terms.
- A friend cancels on me, and it allows me the choice to extend grace and have the deeper conversation.
- I have an argument with my spouse, and it brings us closer as we choose to communicate at a different level.

It is all about choices. All of these choices allow me to rise out of my shadows and to see how my life is working for me. Choosing gratitude and finding the blessing and what makes me better opens up the secret to living in my light and moving forward!

I remember telling my husband, Mark, "When I stay focused on the positive and am in gratitude to God for all our blessings, we do better, things go smoother, life is more enjoyable." He started to experience it too and joined me in shifting.

This is all a precursor to 2020, when my most expansive shift began. Understandably, this shift was in the works the whole time, but this was the point at which I again became conscious of the magnitude of the shift. It was time!

I told myself that I would become a yoga teacher when I turned fifty, but I put it off. I wasn't ready. In 2020, I turned fifty-three years old. It was time to see myself again. I was ready!

I started searching for classes nearby so that I could become a certified yoga instructor. And the world shut down! Yes! That was the fuel I needed. It was time to show up! I became *determined to embolden the light wherever darkness tried to creep in.*

From March to May, while everyone sheltered in, my husband and I updated the guest suites I had run for the past eight years. We refreshed them and breathed new life into them. I also signed up for an online yoga teacher training, and in May 2020 I began the journey of becoming a yogi! June through September 2020 I started my reiki training in Tulsa, Oklahoma. I drove six hours for each nine-hour course, stayed with friends while there, and drove home the next day. July 2020 I started teaching yoga as part of my practicum, and I reopened my guest suites. I hosted more guests in those last few months of 2020 than I had in the previous eight years combined. August 2020 I graduated as a certified yoga instructor! October 2020 I created and opened my healing arts studio, Zia, My Retreat, in quaint, little ol' New Haven, Missouri. Population: 2,089.

It was autumn of 2020 when I started hearing God's plan for me to lead retreats. I had considered this idea for a while but put it in a future plan, a future space. However, one day while I was in my prayer chair conversing with God, it became very evident the retreats were supposed to start ... now! God showed me that I had the space right there in my studio. I started hosting "Solitude and Solidarity" seasonal retreats in 2021 with great success. Small group retreats themed around each season, designed to meet each retreatant in their season of life and help them open and shift into their purpose.

God inspired it. I created it. People came!

Beautiful humans come to Zia to commune, to be seen and to heal. They are met with love. They are seen. They are heard. They lovingly shift! It is a serene and powerful space, oozing with healing energy.

I am shifting at all times and trust greater things are coming! I am consciously aware in each moment that God has a plan and a path waiting. My part is to live in gratitude, which illuminates the path. I can still visit the shadows, as there is no such thing as perfection in this lifetime. However, I know the way back. I can choose to shift into gratitude and into my light, and I do! I embolden the light wherever the darkness tries to creep in.

---

[1] Kairos (Ancient Greek: καιρός) is an ancient Greek word meaning "the right, critical, or opportune moment".

Hi! I am Laura Kohnen. I am just the girl next door who looked my shadows in the face and chose to step into my light! I am the daughter of my amazing Creator, wife to the humble and strong man God gifted me twenty-eight years ago, and mom to three huge-hearted, sassy young women.

I am a creative soul who is nourished through prayer, being in nature, and breathing life into other souls. All of this magic happens at a sweet place called Zia, New Haven, and the soon-to-be Zia, Hermann. Zia, a place where people can stay, retreat, practice yoga, receive reiki, find solitude and solidarity, and reclaim their soul and peace of mind. Zia is the space for shifting! I ask you to join me as we shift into our light and embolden the light of the world around us!

www.ziamyretreat.com/
www.facebook.com/ziamyretreat
www.facebook.com/ziamyretreat.guestsuites
www.instagram.com/ziamyretreat/

KYLE E. WALSH

Don't Be a Sad Story

*"You're under arrest!" I could hear them shouting,
but I was beyond man's law.*

I ran faster, trying to break through. I wanted to get to Petco so I could die among the animals. This was of the upmost importance. I had to run faster. A sudden stab of pain, and then another, until I went stiff as a board and fell forward, struck by a taser. As I was being handcuffed, the only thing I could say was, "Please don't hurt me anymore."

I had the ideal childhood. A loving family, we ate dinner together with no TV and didn't mind. Dad coached all my teams in different sports. He was my hero. However, not even he could protect me from junior high school.

Overweight and sweaty, I was flooded with feelings that scared me, so I cried and listened to music every night, experiencing my first dose of anxiety and depression but didn't know it. Bullied because of my weight and sweat, girls and guys called me "fat." These were supposed to be *my* friends. "You need to get a bra or don't take your shirt off," said one of the girls. I was suicidal in junior high school. The abuse was too much for me. I always lost my temper, went into rages, screamed, and cried. Part of the décor in my bedroom were holes I'd punched in the walls. I wanted out.

"Why suffer this misery?" I thought, but I didn't act on it. I told only one girl. She advised me to talk to our youth ministers. I decided to take a different route. I would make myself popular by being a party guy.

I started binge drinking every weekend, and it worked. I was accepted and invited to the best parties. I got tall and ripped. My love life changed. All of a sudden all the girls who didn't want to *ruin our friendship* paid attention to me. Senior year was amazing, but I had no idea how good life could be until I got to college.

I joined the top fraternity on campus—the best decision I ever made. I instantly made friends who, to this day, I count on for support. These are lifelong friends who have seen my worst and still call me brother.

Those four years were incredible, albeit not without signs of trouble. A close friend took my parents aside to tell them that everyone was worried something might be wrong with me. My parents figured it was my temper, which I'd been battling all my life. But my grades were great, and I always pulled through, so it was never addressed. I continued suffering bouts of anxiety and depression, not knowing what was wrong with me, and spent many manic nights at the bar.

Then it was over. One day, everyone graduated and left. I was staying for law school and everyone else was leaving. I had my first real heartbreak when my girlfriend broke up with me the night before my first day of law school. She was gone. My friends, my support system, all gone. None of my courses prepared me for overwhelming depression.

Drowning in heartbreak and despair, I didn't take law school seriously. I'd cram the night before exams and expect things would be fine. I ended up near the bottom of the class. My innate social anxiety got worse. Time for another transformation!

To be a trial lawyer, I had to be tough. So, K-Wal—the newest version of me—was born. K-Wal was arrogant, vicious. I started working out, lifting weights, and running. I still missed classes, but with great notes and outlines from fellow students, I did well the rest of law school.

I got the dream job I wanted practicing criminal law. I was living in St. Louis, Missouri. One of my bosses became a big brother and mentor. I got a dog. I was a great success. Except for blackouts every weekend, and that time I embarrassed the firm at a nice outdoor bar and restaurant in Clayton, Missouri. No memory, just a few flashes. Others remembered and informed me I'd been drinking all day at a pool before ending up alone at the bar where I was picking fights and yelling so loud that two separate lawyers who were there called my boss the next day and told him. He was upset. I was upset. My mentor was very concerned. He almost called my parents.

Something electric clicked in my brain. I felt a rush of pure energy flowing through me. Suddenly, everything in the universe was perfect. I could quit worrying. I had entered *mania*. It was powerful. I felt unstoppable, like I could be or do anything.

My mentor didn't fire me or demand I go to counseling. I made the decision. Trouble was, I was in mania. My therapist didn't realize. She thought I was this positive, wonderful guy with so much wisdom. This fed the mania. I quit drinking because I no longer needed to feel numb. Talking took its place. I couldn't quit talking. My mind was always racing, and I was so fast with witty comebacks, I could take anyone down.

My behavior continued to be questionable. I would disappear hours at a time. I was telling everyone I loved them. I bought a brand-new BMW. I was buying custom suits and shoes from Chicago. The partners wondered, "Where is he getting all this money?" The answer was—all my savings. I blew it all. When confronted, I got angry. I left the firm to start my own firm. I had a potential partner lined up and was looking at real estate in Clayton. I was going to be my own boss. I had never felt better in my life. The universe was showing me the way, and I followed.

Right into *The Matrix*. I was watching *The Matrix* when everything started to melt. My mania turned into a "psychotic break[1]" in which Trinity, the lead female character in the movie, became my therapist. I loved her soul. I hallucinated and knew without doubt I was a son of God. This was important. Everyone had to know. I made a spectacle of myself so people would read my writings which, by the way, were a rambling, incoherent mess.

Everyone can be like Jesus, like I am. They'll see there's a way. I had to die for the sake of others. I started throwing electronics in the bathtub but stopped when I realized it might start a fire. I gathered different pills and took all of them. I drank calcium lime remover. I stripped naked, even removing my contact lenses. I

---

1 A psychotic break involves a loss of contact with reality characterized by hallucinations (generally auditory type), delusions (ideas in which it is believed with great conviction despite its incoherence), or alterations in language.

vomited, then sliced both wrists up to the forearm. I remember chastising myself for not cutting deeper. My dog was drenched in vomit and blood. It was everywhere. I had a whole host of hallucinations, encouraging me on.

I was running out of time. I slipped on blood and felt weaker, but it only strengthened my resolve. I wrote simple math equations in blood on the wall to explain my psychotic message before I died.

Time to make a scene. I went into the halls of my apartment complex and grabbed two fire extinguishers. One I threw through a plate-glass window of a bar. I was told the surveillance footage caught me entering. Then I lay on the ground, thinking I was finally going to die. But since I didn't, I decided to create more chaos by discharging the other fire extinguisher in the middle of a busy city street.

I ran back to the apartment to check on my dog, slamming into my door thinking I could pass through it. I could do anything! My dog was alive but scared. I loved her, but I had to do this for mankind. Naked, covered in vomit and blood, I start running again. I had to get to Petco to die among the animals. I ran faster, then I saw police cars approaching . . .

What followed were psychiatric hospitals and the help I desperately needed. Diagnosed Bipolar 1, with manic depressive, psychotic symptoms, acute anxiety, and agoraphobia, it took years to get the right combination of medicine. Ultimately, I underwent ECT (shock therapy). I made a promise to myself, "If this somehow works, you will never let bipolar beat you. You will not be a sad story. You will never give up."

I stayed true to my intention. I addressed my alcoholism. I finally fulfilled my dream of owning a law firm, The Walsh Defense. I'm sober, the medicine is working, and I glide around the courtroom with ease. Not with the false confidence of mania or alcohol, but with experience and discipline. I didn't think I could get here, but I did. It took intention, goal setting, discipline, and my commitment. My message to *myself and others:* "Don't be a sad story. Never give up, no matter how dark it seems."

Kyle E. Walsh graduated from the University of Missouri with a Bachelor of Arts degree in Communication and a minor in Political Science. Following completion of his undergraduate studies, Kyle was accepted into the University of Missouri–School of Law where he earned his Juris Doctorate. Kyle began his law practice in St. Louis, Missouri, where he practiced for four years primarily as a criminal defense attorney. In 2010, Kyle returned to his hometown of Poplar Bluff, Missouri, to continue his law practice. Kyle formed his own firm, Walsh Defense, to focus solely on criminal defense. At forty-one, Kyle has been featured in *Missouri Lawyers Weekly* multiple times for his successes. He strives to be the best attorney in Southeast Missouri and beyond. His personal story is an inspiration to many who suffer from mental illness. His motto is: "Don't give up, no matter how dark it is."

www.walshdefense.com
Kwal@walshdefense.com
www.facebook.com/kyle.walsh.1217

TONIA ENGLERT

Losing Her, Finding Me

It is hard to pinpoint an exact moment when I looked in the mirror
and did not recognize who was looking back.

She was a wife, a mother, a friend, a therapist. Mostly, she looked exhausted from all the running away from or striving toward something.

I was living a normal life. I'd get up, get ready, get the kids ready and out the door to school and daycare drop-offs, work all day, pick up everyone, make dinner, do laundry, give baths, put the kids to bed, and spend a few rare moments with the husband. Sleep. Repeat.

Our family was hitting another milestone. We were buying our first home. Our place, with our two kids. Waiting in the wings, a whole new set of milestones was about to start.

It was move-in day. Despite the exhaustion of daily life, I was excited and energized that the day had finally come. We would have room to spread out as our family grew, a place to make memories with our kids. We were almost through unloading the endless supply of boxes and furniture. The helpers were leaving for the day. Then my mom asked if she could talk with me.

"Tonia, I have a doctor's appointment this week. I found some blood in my stool and they want me to do a colonoscopy, just to check things out."

My stomach clenched at her words but then eased as I saw her relaxed demeanor, as if we were talking about going shopping.

I didn't put much thought into that moment, but in hindsight, she had already been showing me what it looked like to lean into faith. Our journey through cancer was a roller coaster with doctor's appointments, multiple surgeries, treatment after treatment, and just enough hope to make up for each devastating update. No matter what they did, the cancer just kept moving and coming back.

With a background in healthcare, I have watched a lot of people die, both from physical illness and mental illness. Mom chose to let her cancer fuel her life, and watching her journey was inspiring. She kept working. Playing with grandkids. She celebrated on a chemo break with her toes in the water at the zero-mile marker in the Florida Keys. She attended mass every week despite the advancement of her cancer.

People would say, "You don't look like you have cancer."

Her response, "Well that's because only part of me is sick." She told us early on that mindset was key and she trusted God. He had a path for her. Well, that path led us down the road to the cancer spreading from her colon to her liver and then to her lungs.

That was my breaking point. I fell to my knees in front of her as she cradled my head in her lap, asking, "Why you? You are a good person, you love everyone, why you?"

She waited until I calmed, cupped her hands around my face, and whispered, "Now, baby, I have had a chance to raise my babies. Every day there is a woman out there fighting to raise theirs. It is just my time."

Funny how words can make you feel so small. In that moment I was a thirty-two-year-old woman, selfishly stomping her three-year-old foot because I just wanted Mom to be around to keep raising me, to welcome another baby on the way, to dance at her grandkids' weddings and to have long talks while working in the garden.

One Saturday morning she asked me to call our priest. I panicked, thinking she was going to ask for last rights, but I did as she asked. The priest came and, after what seemed like forever, said, "Paulette, why did you ask me here?"

Mom responded, "I just need to talk."

"I'll leave you two," I said, and started to leave the room.

"You need to stay," she insisted.

"Paulette, are you afraid of dying?" the priest asked.

The room was still. I watched as mom raised her eyes and met each of ours directly. When she spoke, her voice was strong. She finished with such intensity, each word felt like a caress. "I am not afraid to die. I know where I am going. I am sad at what I am going to miss."

She wasn't afraid to die. She leaned into her faith until the very end, allowing our family to care for her until her last breath, surrounded by people who loved her.

Then life resumes, right? Except for the huge piece that is missing.

To avoid the pain and deep hurt, I did what I was so good at—striving and running. Striving in my career, to be the best wife, mother, and volunteer. I kept busy because busy meant I didn't have to acknowledge the chasm in my heart, a hole that nothing could fill. I pretended that everything was OK when I really felt broken. When I slowed long enough to glance in the mirror, the woman looking back wasn't someone I recognized at all.

This pattern lasted for about a year. God knew I couldn't have done it much longer. One cold, dreary Saturday morning, I was in bed weeping, bereft with grief, when I heard a little knock on the door.

My youngest daughter, Ellie, entered. "Momma, is your heart sad?"

I responded, "Yes, my heart is missing Oma" (their word for their grandmother).

"It's OK, Momma. When your heart is sad, and you have tears, that's when she is the closest to you." Her words opened a door into the next chapter of my life, a chapter in which I found hope.

In that moment I felt a loving presence, an embrace, I like to think from my mom, or God. That embrace shifted something in me. I felt *held in my grief*. I wasn't alone. My mom walked through some of her darkest days with God, and I knew He was there to help me hold my grief.

I knew I needed help, so I made a phone call to the hospice social worker who had cared for our family, and I told her I hit the bottom of my grief. She suggested counseling. I balked. That didn't feel right. She then suggested a silent retreat at the Mercy Center. That is where I finally went to lay down my striving and running, to just be still and let the thoughts that were racing around in my head come out on paper.

What came out was anger. Anger is not an emotion I do well (another book, perhaps). I was angry at my mom for being OK with leaving, and I was angry at God for taking her. In this setting, stillness embraced me with grace, forgiveness, and love. My body and mind felt lighter. My cold spirit kindled into flame.

That silent retreat led to many others, first as a way to escape the striving and running, then just to experience quiet time with God, where I listened, asking what my next steps might be on my healing journey. It also led me into Spiritual Direction. First as a directee, and now in school to become a Spiritual Director myself. To sit with others in holy listening.

Upon reflection, my family may have appeared a little crazy. Things that seemed important before didn't hold the same weight anymore. I left a toxic job without a definite plan in place, trusting that God would guide us through. We sold a perfectly good house to chase a dream of starting a business. Guess what? We have a roof over our heads and a business that is thriving during a pandemic. I have a family who values time with each other over material possessions. We have a deep faith and know that no matter what is thrown at us, blessings will abound.

Like others who've embarked on a healing journey, I had no clue where it would lead. I have learned to behold the messiness of the journey, to share it, then learn to sit with it until the real thing, the real emotion, surfaces. Then I face it, no matter how ugly, no matter how painful. Running may have seemed easier, but in the end it just intensified the pain.

Now when I look in the mirror, I see a woman who loves to learn, loves her faith, loves to laugh and to go on adventures, and loves spending time with people and listening to their stories. A woman starting to get a glimpse of who she was intended to be, the one God created, before the junk of life piled up and clouded the view.

This healing journey has given me hope that I can move forward with something more than surviving and striving, that I can thrive! I have hope that blessings will flow from the experiences in life that cause the greatest pain, and if we let them, they will forever change the trajectory of our lives. I miss my mom, but the search is on to find myself, knowing that in losing her, I am finding me.

Tonia Englert was born and raised in Hermann, Missouri. She currently resides with her husband, Jeff, and three children: Sabryn, Ellie, and Braeden. She was in the medical field for over twenty-five years, primarily treating patients as an Occupational Therapy Assistant in a variety of settings. She left the clinical setting a few years ago to work alongside her husband running their family business, J & T Trailers, while pursuing her own vision of becoming a Spiritual Director. Tonia is actively engaged as a speaker and author, committed to sharing her healing faith journey. Her goal is to model, encourage, and inspire others to confidently walk their personal journey of faith.

www.facebook.com/tonia.englert
www.instagram.com/toniae76/
www.linkedin.com/in/tonia-englert-5b5173a3/

Coffee

She gave me something I didn't want, and never needed.

I had never even been introduced to this idea until I met her. It was never a part of my life, and I liked it that way. Part of me thinks she introduced me on purpose. She wanted to see me struggle so she could be the savior, even though she never fulfilled that destiny. She made it a competition, too, which was the worst part. She's always been like that, though. She loves the chase. The chase of the competition, the thrill, the uncertainty. That's how she's always been. She made me believe not only that the only exercising that counted was when I burned at least five-hundred calories, but that meals no longer existed. She made me believe that if I wasn't spending every waking moment of my day exercising, then it was not a day worth living. When I did decide to "eat" in front of her, it was coffee. It's an appetite suppressant and only five calories. She taught me that trick.

She never forgot to let me know how many days it had been since she last ate. I beat her every time, though, but I wanted her to feel worthy. I let her believe that three days of not eating was a feat, when, really, I was going on eight. She made me believe that the thing looking back at me in the mirror would never measure up, until there was nothing to measure up to, until my body got so thin that there was almost nothing looking back at me. She made me hate these mirrors, and the conversations I had with them. She loved mirrors, though. She's always been vain. Every time she passed one, she'd lift her shirt, just enough to see her stomach, then she'd look right at me as if to let me know that that should have been part of my daily routine all along. But I guess if I looked like her, I would be vain too.

I ran eight miles every single day. I always hated running, but for some reason, I fell in love with it. Maybe it was because my body felt lighter, since my meals consisted of coffee nowadays. I was always amazed by my body at this point in time; I never really felt faint, even when I hadn't eaten for eight days prior. I ran fast too. My mom had always been a runner, and I nearly lapped her. It wasn't enough, though. She supposedly went to three spin classes every single day, burning fifteen-hundred calories. She wouldn't forget to let me know that she passed out in the middle of class too. Was this true? I'm sure it wasn't, but she told me it was. My eight miles now weren't good enough. Since I didn't pass out, it wasn't enough. None of my clothes fit me anymore, but I loved it. I started to fall in love with the chase, and I hated myself for it.

No one really intervened. I don't know if I wanted them to, though. I got a new job in the middle of the pandemic driving cars to and from dealerships, 7:00 a.m. to 7:00 p.m. I worked for my dad, and he always encouraged me to take a "lunch break," because he knew. He knew my secret that I thought I was keeping so well. He would hand me his credit card every lunch break and tell me to go wherever I wanted and to get whatever I wanted. I would just take his card and drive myself to the nearest gas station, where I would consume the infamous five-calorie meal: coffee. I would return his card and tell him that I ate in the car. He didn't ask any questions. I wasn't around him or my mom enough for them to say anything. My mom always made comments about how skinny I was, but it was only because she was on her own weight-loss journey. These comments, of course, made me want to keep going. Maybe I should have just told my mom the secret to the ultimate weight loss.

I wondered how I had gotten to this point; how had I let her have this much sway and power over me? It was embarrassing, frankly, but I felt like she liked me more. She gave me more attention when I was skinnier. I think what I loved most was that she was worried about me. No one has ever been worried about me. It was always me, worried about other people. I was dying to be taken care of, and this was a surefire way to be taken care of. She loved my new body. Or at least, that's how I took it. She would tell me that I couldn't get too thin because she needed something to hug. It was also this point in time that we were more than friends. Much, much more. It seemed like me becoming the thinnest version of myself was something that bonded us. So I thought that meant that if we were to continue being more than friends, I needed to continue starving. I liked where we were headed, so I continued my black coffee meals. We had a bond unlike any other bond I had ever had before. She was my best friend.

You may be wondering how a person could have this much dominance over another person. I'm not completely sure either, but it was like a drug. Her love for the chase manifested itself into me, and it was something I was not proud of. What she stood for, and the person she is, was something I never was, and never will be. I looked at old photos of myself and realized that I was much, much happier when I was not *skinny*. I got to the point where the only thing on my mind was food: how long I could make it without eating; if I could still exercise that day without passing out; if I could get away with not eating in a social setting. It consumed me. I spent a lot of time looking at photos, comparing my past self with my current self. I looked at photos where I thought I was "fat," when, really, I was extremely thin. I think this was my turning point, realizing that my "fat" self was actually a very healthy weight, and a *happier* weight.

Honestly, I'm not really sure what the exact shift was. I simply realized I was missing out. I was missing out on the "family dinner night" my roommates and I hosted every Tuesday. I was missing out on my own birthday cake because I was afraid of sugar. I was simply missing out. I was tired of food and exercise occupying my every thought and action, so I let myself eat. I found a new love for cooking that I hadn't had before. I used to love breakfast, and I realized I really hadn't had breakfast in a long, long time. I started with breakfast, then lunch. I would get excited about coming home to cook something for myself, even if it was just an egg. I tried to romanticize every meal by sitting down at the table and truly enjoying my food.

When it came to exercise, my body hurt so bad from working it so hard, it was almost detrimental when I took my first off day. I told myself that I would go during the week but that I could take the weekend off. And when I was working out, I did it for the sole benefit of myself, and my own wellbeing, not as a punishment of any sort. I forgot what it was like to exercise and be able to push myself. I'd gotten so used to focusing on not passing out during a workout that I had forgotten what my body was capable of. I fell back in love with the idea of it, and if I wanted to go on an occasional Saturday or Sunday run, I let myself. I slowly relearned to join the family dinners, eat the birthday cake, and maybe put cream in my coffee.

Of course, there is a part of me that still struggles with the balance between it all. Some comments spin me in the wrong direction. There may always be a part of me that misses that version of myself, the one that was holding on for dear life, petrified someone might find out the secret. She knew, of course, since she was the teacher of the secret. Ironically, she became one of my favorite people to share meals with. I used to not be able to eat in front of her, but now we chose to make exquisite concoctions together. Perhaps it wasn't my "skinny" that she had liked, but me.

I do still take my coffee black, but only for the aesthetic.

Sydney Zografos found her love for writing recently, as she was reluctantly convinced by her roommate that she should pursue a career in such. When she is not writing, Sydney loves capturing candid photos with disposable cameras, listening to any sort of music she can get her hands on, and moving her body. She is currently wrapping up her undergraduate career at Rockhurst University with a BA in English and Psychology and a minor in General Business. She plans on purchasing a one-way ticket to Europe after graduation, with hopes of starting her own record company, becoming a published author in *The New York Times*, and being a speech pathologist . . . all in due time.

sydneynzografos@gmail.com
www.instagram.com/sydzog/
www.linkedin.com/in/sydney-zografos-836411196/

Prisoner of My Past

Hi there, my name is Amy Rivera,
and I'm a recovering prisoner of my past.

You may know me as the "the beauty queen with the big leg" or hear about my accolades in the lymphatic community, but today I wanted to share the dark side of my life with you, the one I've kept secret until now.

I was born with a rare disease that caused swelling on the right side of my body—from my ears to my toes. I grew up in isolation, constantly being told I was weird, ugly, or—the best one—that I would never amount to anything. That last one was the story I picked to hide behind, as awful as that sounds.

My parents divorced after years of my father's drug abuse and infidelity. My mother worked tirelessly to make ends meet, but she finally broke. I was eight years old. The family secrets were about to come out as my mother lost herself.

Imagine this: *an eight-year-old daughter and her two younger siblings sharing a hotel bed, all facing the wall, while her mother has a threesome on the floor. Even though we could not see what was happening, we heard every sound.*

At nine years old, my mother remarried, and I was forced to be a part of another family—all strangers to me. All of a sudden, I had a stepbrother and stepsister. The strange man my mother married after only being divorced for six months ended up being a sex addict.

I felt the walls caving in. I panicked whenever my friends were around. Being a child of swingers wasn't something I wanted the world to know. I was suffering from extreme anxiety and low self-worth, but I didn't know that at the time. Sex was the pinnacle of our household. I felt so ashamed.

When I was fifteen years old, I came home and told my parents about my first sexual encounter. I was given a high five and told, "you won't get pregnant when you swallow." I swallowed more than that; I swallowed my soul and self-respect. I wasn't any better than the people I despised.

At seventeen, I experienced an identity crisis. I turned toward school to get away from my home life, only to get bullied. I was tired of being called "the girl with the elephant leg." I hated my life. I wanted to escape the shame of dysfunction.

I knew I had to be the one who stood up for myself. So, one day, I stopped saying "sorry for the way I am" and started declaring "this is who I am." I took that courage to the stage in 1999, winning the Miss Junior America Hostess title. My first victory in a lifelong battle.

I got pregnant when I was eighteen. It didn't matter what I thought about having the baby. My mother forced me to have an abortion, then she went on to tell the entire family about it. Have you ever walked into a room and had everyone staring at you with disgust? Disgust was a feeling I recognized deep down. I felt it when I looked into the mirror. I never admitted how much pain this caused, but my life was never the same. My crown was stored in a box from that day forward. I didn't deserve it.

I found myself in the same position at the age of nineteen. Once again, my mother tried to force her hand on this unborn child. I decided she would not ruin my life again, and I moved out to save this child's life, and my own.

I graduated high school, bought a new car, rented an apartment, and worked two jobs. There was no way I was going to fail. I was going to be what I set out to be, and that was a successful, intelligent woman of worth.

At the age of twenty, I received a phone call that haunts me to this day. "Amy, your grandmother was shot." I held the phone in silence. I couldn't believe what I'd heard on the other end! I handed the phone off and sat back down at the dinner table in complete shock. My grandfather had shot my grandmother eight times.

My grandmother's affair, my grandfather's sick and twisted parenting, my aunt's suicide, the albino cousin that nobody wanted to talk about, the great aunt who went missing, and, of course, the years of incest were all too much to bear.

I'd seen and experienced things that will forever haunt me. PTSD became my lifelong companion. It was clear what I was meant to do. I had to break the *chains of dysfunction*.

By learning from all I've endured, my experience, wisdom, knowledge, and resilience can be used to help others. By embracing forgiveness for others, I was able to break the chains of dysfunction. By forgiving myself, I was able to accept my own emotional and spiritual well-being.

I had to learn that *I am a woman of worth*. None of us are born "strong." We develop this strength through the challenges of life. Although we don't always remain on the same path, there will be times we are called to persevere in areas we'd rather not walk. That's the complexity of life. All my paths intersected at *forgiveness* to show me my purpose: to help others heal as I heal myself.

It doesn't matter how healing looks, but it must be intentional. This is the starting point with mental health recovery, or as I call it, "being a prisoner of the past." For my healing journey, I started creating intention through what I most lacked in my life—wellness.

I asked myself, "What would life look like if I were free from generational trauma, survivor's guilt, internal pain, and self-doubt. There was no going back to my old life after envisioning my future life with happiness, laughter, and good health. I knew this would be an emotional and physical roller coaster, but it was worth the ride to happiness! I threw myself into self-education, surrounded myself with the type of people I wanted to learn from, and, most importantly, cut off anything and everything that held me down. Yes, even family members. I knew at the age of eight I wanted to help heal others, I just didn't know how until I focused on my *why*. Little did I know, the *why* was with me the entire time. I just had to heal to see it.

Today, I share my *why* with people who need to hear they are not alone.

Opening that door allowed me to realize I love my life. My energy is vital. I'm calm and peaceful. I am committed to expressing gratitude throughout this fantastic journey. I make myself a priority. I see a therapist who can help me navigate the trauma I've experienced. I reconnect with people I enjoy being around. I embrace the excitement of life's adventures.

I'm ready to use my past experiences as the vehicle to guide others through their healing process. My purpose in life is to be the light for those in the darkness. As you finish reading this chapter of my life, I hope it helps you turn a new page in yours. Shift with intention.

Amy Rivera created a blueprint for success. Born with primary lymphedema, a disease that causes tissue swelling in extremities due to an accumulation of fluid, Amy spent much of her life with a right leg that was 200 percent larger than her left leg. Finally, in 2013, after having been misdiagnosed for more than thirty years, Rivera was properly diagnosed and underwent the first in a series of surgeries that reduced the circumference of her leg and eventually removed thirty-five pounds of trapped fluid. Last fall, she published a book about her experiences, *Drop the Skirt: How My Disability Became My Superpower.* She is also making a difference through her nonprofit, *Ninjas Fighting Lymphedema Foundation,* which assists fellow patients. Amy Rivera & Associates, her for-profit company, became the exclusive North American distributor for Fast n' Go bandages, the most efficient hybrid bandages on the market for lymphedema treatment.

www.amyrivera.com/
www.winourfight.org/
www.hybridbandaging.com/

JULIE LAWSON

The Intuitive No

I am a yes woman.

I say yes to everything: requests for help, donations, meetings, events, overtime, volunteering, career opportunities, and even food (especially chocolate). I have always been this way. Because I want to be, because I think others want me to be, and because I appreciate the inherent and unexpected opportunities in "yes."

"Yes" works for me. It has led me down astonishing paths: to singing and acting on stages all over the country; to being a radio DJ, TV personality, and podcaster; to being an entrepreneur; and to being a published author. "Yes" took me from my own traumatic experience with a violent assault to advocating at the local and national levels on behalf of victims. It unexpectedly led me to a career in nonprofit management and to a second career in leadership development coaching and consulting. "Yes" has led me to jungles and deserts, to hurricanes and high rises, to the tops of mountains and the depths of seas. I have had amazing (and not-so-amazing) adventures, met remarkable people, studied religions and languages, and discovered the beauty of the human experience, simply because I said "yes."

Saying "yes" helped me pursue a career dedicated to finding meaningful interventions and solutions for some of the most difficult social issues facing our communities. My career has been wonderful, rewarding, frustrating, hopeful, conflicted, and simultaneously powerful and humbling. And even when I felt myself waning after many years, I said "yes" to people and experiences I knew would push me past my capabilities because I was asked to help a community hurting from crime, violence, and inequity. Finally, after twenty years, I felt burned out and exhausted. The gravity of my work was weighing heavily on me, and I no longer felt effective. So, in 2017 I said "yes" to myself and launched my own consulting firm, hoping this fresh perspective and new work would cure me of my midlife malaise.

Though this new start was exhilarating, I quickly felt as exhausted and ineffective as before. Instead of feeling interesting and exciting, a lifetime of yeses was starting to feel chaotic and stressful. By 2021 I was juggling multiple clients, navigating a global pandemic (and related business losses), helping care for sick family members, managing my own serious health issues, and mourning the untimely deaths of several loved ones. I was bending over backward to appease others, often too tired to defend myself against unwarranted criticism or demands. My relationships were strained (or failing), my life felt out of control, my body was rebelling, and my mind was uncharacteristically scattered. I lived in a state of inexplicable tension, exhaustion, and unproductiveness. And yet, though it was no longer working for me, I continued to say yes.

I kept going like this, using the reserve fumes in my tank until I sputtered to a stop. I suddenly only had the strength or focus for the next step in front of me. I excelled at mindfulness not by choice but by necessity. I existed in a feeling of unsettling stillness that, over time, smoothed out into acceptance. And that's when I heard the Intuitive No.

One afternoon I was talking with a friend about this new state of exhausted stillness. My life felt like it had gone off the rails, and I desperately wanted to feel normal again. More importantly, I wanted to feel happy. She suggested if I could just reset myself to my factory settings, I'd find my happiness again. I nodded. That sounded right. I just needed to engage in the thoughts and behaviors that would bring me back to who I had always been. It might not be easy, but surely it was simple enough. From somewhere deep within I heard a quiet, firm voice say, "no."

No?

"No. You can't go back. That's not you anymore."

I was stunned. What was this strange resistance? Who was saying it? And *why* was she saying it? It felt like I was no longer trying to fool my inner compass. I could feel—and accept—the direction I was meant to go with clarity and conviction. Somewhere, in the throes of heartache and disruption, my soul had shifted into a better version of itself. My mind just hadn't recognized it yet.

My joy had always come from serving others, from pursuing tough but meaningful challenges, and from making those I love happy. (It still does.) Like many of us, I didn't often consider what I wanted because what I wanted was for *others* to be fulfilled. That was me. Until it wasn't. I had forgotten to take myself along on this journey toward happiness. To admit I wasn't fulfilled in my life—and that I felt this at a deep, existential level—was earth-shattering. It was taking its toll. It was time to listen to what my intuition said about what I should do, who I should interact with, and what would make me truly happy.

I started paying attention to the people and circumstances that created the most tension within me. I was surprised by how often I felt it. That tension was my intuition saying, "no," "not yet," or "that's not who you are." When something was right, it felt so. There was no tension, no reluctance. Little by little this intuitive voice became louder, offering me information and guidance when I needed it most. I said "no" to the client who had been taking advantage of my skills and flexibility. I said "no" to the friend who didn't respect me fully. I said "no" to the projects that were robbing me of time and energy but weren't providing growth or happiness. I said "no" to shortchanging myself when it mattered most. And I said "no" to anything that no longer served me.

I admit I expected some fallout from my new practice of saying "no." But it turns out that, when it's an Intuitive No, pushback doesn't matter. You are simply on the path that is right for you. I have learned that intuition is quiet, sure-footed, and direct. It does not waver. If it isn't listened to, it will surround you with tension until you choose the right direction. We can ignore it, but it will just continue to nudge. We can fight it, but like a toddler throwing a tantrum, the harder we fight, the more exhausted, frustrated, and resentful we become. Like a good parent, intuition will patiently hold us until we give in.

I'd love to say my story of transformation came upon traversing the Grand Canyon, saving someone's life, or following a life-altering incident (I have experienced all these things and, for the most part, they just left me hungry, bewildered, or tired). Life tends to hit us like earthquakes: either one catastrophic event that changes everything in a moment, or, as in my case, a series of small, pulsing shifts that change our landscape over time.

These small pulses led me to understand what was right for me. Now I seek those moments, relationships, and opportunities that feel in alignment with what I want and who I am. If I feel that familiar tension, I examine it and, most often, walk away. I have learned that service to others, in the way that utilizes the best of myself, is only possible when it is fully aligned with my highest purpose. "Yes" should come easily, quickly, and without hesitation because we know we are the right person at the right time with the right skills, and because we have a desire to serve in this capacity. This is only possible when we clear the way for what is right by saying "no."

I have experienced significant hardship, illness, violence, and heartaches that have become beautiful lessons of faith, strength, and wisdom. But none have been as powerful as learning to listen to the voice within that says, "*No. That's not for you.*" Intuition is a gift that, if we listen, will guide us to the greatest moments life has to offer. And those moments are where true happiness lives.

Julie H. Lawson has served as a nonprofit executive and entrepreneur for more than twenty-five years. She is currently CEO of Reins Institute, a leadership development firm providing customized leadership development programs. Prior to launching Reins Institute, Julie led a team assisting thousands of victims with trauma-informed services, during which time she built her foundation of research and knowledge regarding trauma, crisis, and resilience. Julie has trained more than three thousand individuals in emotional intelligence and resilience strategies. She has served as the inaugural Executive Director of the Missouri Supreme Court's Commission on Racial and Ethnic Fairness, Executive Director of the Crime Victim Center, and currently serves as Executive Director of the Association of VA Hematology/Oncology. She is a recognized expert in women's leadership issues and is the founder of the National Alliance for Victims. Her purpose in life is to gather and spread stories of grit and grace. Julie's book, *Warrior Principles: 8 Rules for a Resilient Life,* will be released in Fall 2022 alongside the *Warrior Principles Podcast.*

www.linkedin.com/in/jhlawson
www.facebook.com/jhlawson
www.twitter.com/juliehlawson
www.reinsinstitute.com

NICK LAMIA

Intention with Heart

Your mind will do everything it takes to attain
the dream where the most energy is spent.

When it came to hockey and school, I was not gifted. I was always small for my age, and only an average student. But I did have a different kind of gift. I knew the importance of creating clear goals and dreams at an early age.

Do most children have goals and dreams? Many don't, including some of the kids I coach. At least they're not written down or drawn on a vision board. I created a vision-board party last year for my team. A third of the team showed up. Some parents did not want to introduce vision boards to their children because they felt it added unnecessary pressure, setting them up for failure. I believe that not having a vision board is setting them up for failure.

I had dreams for my future. From an early age I had a strong desire to play hockey. My path would take me from college hockey to pro hockey, and eventually to pro hockey in Denmark. It was an exciting adventure, and it came with invaluable life lessons. In my case, these were lessons I have been able to share with others, to help them grow as individuals and achieve their dreams.

Upon my return from Denmark, I started my own hockey camp with the intention of helping kids understand what it takes to play college and pro hockey in Europe. More than anything, I wanted them to experience what I had just lived. I felt that if I, an undersized, average kid, could do it, anybody could. Playing in front of passionate fans singing songs was incredible. Meeting people from all over the world (Russian coach, roommates from Czech Republic) was priceless!

Although I did not have children of my own yet, I enjoyed working with the kids. Having accomplished my biggest dream—playing pro hockey in Europe—my focus transitioned into helping others achieve their dreams. I knew that teaching a system of intentional steps would help individuals become the best version of themselves.

What started out as a purely tactical approach through camps and coaching soon evolved into educating others on the process that I used to turn my dreams into realities. It was about seeing a bigger picture and using strategies that pertained to their individual situation. As Isaiah Hankel said in *Black Hole Focus*: "First, they realized they needed a purpose. Then, they defined an endpoint for their purpose and worked backwards to fulfill it. . . . This is the exact opposite of what tacticians do. Tactical people let to-do lists guide their lives, as if having meetings and putting out fires will help them fulfill their master plans. Do not fall into this trap. Trickle-forward goal setting does not work."

The Lamia Process: This is for you, Coop!

Your goal is to find your mountain peak, *not* the hiking path you will be using to scale the mountain. *Your mind will do everything it takes to attain the dream where the most energy is spent.*

- **Create an end point (a vision)** and then work backward. For example, my son, Cooper, at eight years old, defined his mountain peak: to play for the Colorado Avalanche. With that start, we can work backward, deciding where he wants to play or go to school to have the highest probability of reaching his mountain peak.

- **Create an action plan.** Run the numbers needed to accomplish your vision. I crafted my hockey skills unknowingly, by accumulating thousands of hours of playing hockey at home. My suggestion for Coop and you, dear reader: get Daniel Coyle's book *The Talent Code: Greatness Isn't Born. It's Grown. Here's How.* This brilliant book teaches the importance of and provides great examples of ***deliberate practice.*** *It's a game changer!* It's the math and science together!

- **Be Disciplined.** This is not just the third step; it is an ongoing step. The word "discipline" gets thrown around pretty casually, but the reality is, discipline does not stand alone; it must be *driven by vision*. Why? Because life will always get in the way. Your motivation and inspiration will wane. As soon as there are setbacks, you will give up, unless you have your goals clearly defined. Use vision boards. Develop action plans. The clearer and more specific you can identify your goals, the better! Will they change? Very likely. But if you drive the change, then it is still part of your plan.

- **Ask why!** At each step in the process, ask yourself, "Why?"
  - Why are those your dreams and goals, and what is your vision?
  - Why do you want this, and how hard are you willing to work to get there?
  - What will it take to achieve your goals? Example: How many hours of deliberate practice do you need to hone your skills, perhaps for a new job? This process is applicable to all professions.
- **Be Open, Make Mistakes, Be Honest and Have Faith:** When I was nine years old, I dreamed of playing college hockey on the East Coast. After many twists and turns, course changes, and having incredible advocates, a coach signed me up to play for Colby College in Maine. Can't get any more East Coast than that. I'm grateful my long-time aspiration of playing hockey on the East Coast finally came true; however, the path that got me there is another chapter in another book. The essential thing for the Lamia Process is to:
  - know you will make mistakes—maybe even really fu!k up—but if you are honest with yourself and others, every mistake will turn into a lesson to help you go forward.
  - be open. Leave room for life to intervene. Be resilient, not rigid.

Change is at the core of being resilient. My mindset shifted, sometimes radically, as I found my way from St. Louis to Culver Military Academy in Indiana, then to Colby College in Maine. The opportunity to play in Europe afforded me the luxury of not only learning about other cultures but truly appreciating them. The wonderful opportunities I've had opened my mind and helped me to grow as a person and to develop the guidelines that I use to help the people I teach and mentor as they work toward achieving their goals.

Purposeful Goals

Both goal setting and dream setting are powerful tools. But it took shifting my mindset to focus on more purposeful goals, not just tangible ones, to truly achieve my purpose.

My advice–**start with Why**. Not an action plan. The sequence is massively important. Ask and understand *why* you want what you want to put yourself on the right path to success. With those first steps in place, the *how* will find its way to you. Then once you have the puzzle pieces in place, self-discipline will follow. As Hankel said, "The message of the story is simple: creating a compelling and tangible vision for your future will pull you towards achieving your goals." When I started on the road to fulfilling my goals and dreams, I had one setback after another, many self-inflicted. My determination to accomplish what I had set out to do was like an invisible force pulling me toward what I wanted.

Now I've added this step to the process: *Set your intention with heart and keep your mind crystal clear on your goals*—the rest is a walk in the park.

After becoming a dad to my son, Coop, I knew what my finish line needed to be. Before I die, I want my son and I to look at each other with unwavering trust, unconditional love, and respect. I want him to feel like I gave everything I had to help him have the best life possible, to teach him life lessons that made me a better person, compassionate, kind to people and animals. Finally, I want him to know that goals must have a higher purpose. They aren't just about me— or you—or him. They have to make a positive difference for others. My life was changed by having guidance and direction. Now I have the skills and experience to help others impact the world in an uplifting way. My reward is knowing I make a difference. As Simon Sinek, *The New York Times* bestselling author and TEDx phenomenon, says, "The goal is not simply for you to cross the finish line, but to see how many people you can inspire to run with you."

For all those whose lives I touch—set your intention with heart and reach for the stars!

Nick Lamia has served as an Edward Jones financial advisor since 1999. He played a key role in expanding the firm's presence in the United Kingdom by opening the first international Edward Jones branch office in Edinburgh, Scotland, where he served clients and mentored fellow financial advisors from 2002 through 2007. He earned an economics degree from Colby College in 1997, his CFP® certificate in 2009, and is a proud alum of Culver Military Academy. His community involvement includes coaching youth teams with the AAA Amateur Blues and Chesterfield Hockey Association. Originally from St. Louis, he and his son, Cooper, live in Town and Country, Missouri. A former professional hockey player, he pays it forward by coaching the St. Louis Knights and is a Humane Policy Volunteer Leader for the United States Humane Society. His vision: "to empower people to do the things that inspire them, so together we can build a better world."

www.facebook.com/nick.lamia1

Be the Light

Life was supposed to be good!

The youngest of four with two wonderful parents, I grew up in a well-structured home. Although we moved all the time, my father stressed "we" as a family, kind of an "us against the world" mission. And it worked beautifully.

In 1985, I decided it was my turn to put my mark on the world. So, after wasting four years of a college education (while learning a lot about people), I joined the United States Navy. My father's mentorship really paid off. Since he had a twenty-four-year career in the Navy, I was prepared for what to expect. Don't get me wrong, the Navy was not easy. But at least I entered with a framework.

I advanced quickly with hard work, faith, and a unique ability to *read* people. I figure folks out pretty quickly, a talent I have to this day. In 2007, I reached the rank of Command Master Chief, and in 2009 I was off to Iraq. I returned in 2010, and that's when things got "interesting."

I met my wife (also a Navy vet) in 2010. It was love at first sight. Although I had been married before, I knew this was "it" from the moment I saw her. We married in 2011 and moved to Missouri in 2012 with my daughter, Catherine. Catherine and my wife became best friends instantly!

In 2015, my wife was diagnosed with liver cancer. Cancer was not a word we often spoke about in the Love family. We had no history of it, and, frankly, after both my wife and I completed our military service, we felt kind of invincible. Then cancer. We listened to the doctors and followed the regimen, thinking that as long as we did, everything would be fine.

In the same year, I was diagnosed with bladder cancer. It was my thirtieth year of military service. What a nice retirement gift! After several years of chemotherapy, the decision was made in September of 2020 to remove my bladder. I had two additional surgeries due to complications.

My wife continued in the fight of her life. She did everything; in fact, she was a great "lab rat" for the doctors because she was in outstanding physical condition, apart from the cancer. She fought hard but eventually lost her battle in February 2021.

The tough times of 2020 defiantly spilled over into 2021. I survived the first thirty days after losing my wife, what I like to call "the Costco phase," which happens after a major event in your life. You receive food gifts from Costco. Don't get me wrong, they are very appreciated. But they are usually perishable items and don't last long. Frankly, it's your first indication that life does go on.

But you don't care about that. All you know is that your wife is gone, people who say they "love" you are gone, and you are truly *alone*! Yes, for the first time in my life I was alone. No wife, no kids, no nothing! My kids were grown at this point and, although they did an outstanding job of checking on me, they had their own lives to live. My wife's family took the opportunity to "ghost" me. In their book, I don't even breathe.

Everyone says they want freedom. Trust me, you don't. Freedom is terrifying! For the first time in my life, I could do anything (or nothing) and it would not matter. All my bills were paid. I had a house and a truck, and no responsibilities to anyone but myself . . . or so I thought. I also had no direction. After all, my whole life had been given directions. My father was in the Navy for twenty-four years, and I served for thirty. You can't ask for more direction than that. After a while you just assume someone is going to tell you what to do.

In April 2021, I heard a calling. I know that sounds strange, but it is true. My wife's voice resonated in my head, "Do something that makes a difference." My wife used to do what she called a "Friday Message" (I still do) where she talked about being kind and loving to one another. I listened to her last recorded message over and over again. She ended it with "Be the light, be the ripple" in someone's life.

I knew she would want me to do something related to cancer that made a difference. This was a very difficult situation. It would have been easy to just write a check every month. But I knew I couldn't get away with that. I had to do more. I had to touch people, I had to raise awareness. I had to be, "boots on the ground." I prayed for an answer.

Then it came to me. It wasn't cancer I could impact. It was everything surrounding it. The travel costs, food costs, lodging costs, and all the other things that have a major impact on the lives of not just the cancer "champion" but their family as well. As much as I wanted to, I could not cure all the forms of cancer, but every family experiences situations and needs requiring assistance.

In May 2021, with $250.00 and a GoFundMe, I started the Be The Light Foundation. I decided I would raise money any way I could. So, I started going door-to-door selling jars of homemade salsa. My neighbors were very kind and were more than happy to purchase them. I also received assistance from a place I didn't expect.

Lucy Roberts, the real estate agent who sold me my home back in 2010, noticed the GoFundMe and jumped at the opportunity to provide the guidance I desperately needed. I will always be indebted to her.

It was not easy. I had no idea what I was doing, and I was still coping with the pain of losing my wife. Be The Light was the right thing to do, if nothing else as a distraction from my grief.

Be The Light started as a two-hours-a-day, three-days-a-week cause. Basically, something to do between streaming movies. But a strange thing happened. I discovered people just like myself—people who watched someone beautiful and healthy one day be torn down the next.

When someone wanted to help, I asked them, "What is the status of your heart? Is it still intact? Do you have hope? Not just hope for the cancer 'champion' but also for yourself? Is the glass half-empty or half-full?"

For most people, the glass was still half-full. All they needed was a little "light." And *hope*!

Be The Light quickly went from hours to days. What was a distraction became a full-time job—a job I welcomed!

Which leads me to what I've learned: we cannot control what happens in our lives. We cannot control who lives or who dies. Who hurts us or who cares about us? Who loves us or who hates us? We are all subject to our experiences. What we can control is how we react to them. It would have been easy for me to crawl up in a ball and shut the world out. And for a while that is exactly what I did. When you lose someone, nothing else matters. And how much you hurt reflects how much you love that person.

Hard questions keep going through your head. "What was the point of loving them if they are just going to leave? What was the point of taking care of them if they are not going to be around to say thank you?"

The point is the person you lost is always a part of you. You continue to take that person forward inside you. The real challenge is how you move forward. I chose to live a positive life. I realized there is nothing more important than the relationship you have with someone. If you focus on the relationship, and not the sale, life gets a whole lot richer. People are basically good. They just need to know you care.

I am still healing. I will be for the rest of my life. I'll keep my glass half-full. I keep her lessons about, love, hope, grace, and kindness with me. I carry her dream with me. It has made me a much better person, and a much better man. I fill the empty half of my glass with positive thoughts and actions as well as great relationships. My glass is overflowing! I have learned that I have the ability to love again, which was unexpected. I have met a wonderful woman, and I look forward to taking the rest of this journey with her. I don't know what my future holds, but I know it will be full of light.

Ceroma Love is founder and president of Be The Light Foundation, a nonprofit organization dedicated to helping families with out-of-pocket costs for patients receiving cancer care. Ceroma served for thirty years in the United States Navy, retiring as a Command Master Chief. He earned his master's degree from Webster University and opened Lion Storm CrossFit in Wentzville, Missouri. He is the father of two: Ceroma III (CJ), who currently serves in the Navy, and Catherine Keyes, a full-time teacher and mom. Drawing on his military experience, his natural ability to cultivate relationships, and his faith, Ceroma has grown Be The Light Foundation from its grassroots beginning into a national organization.

Brightshine1181@gmail.com
www.bethelightindarkness.com
www.facebook.com/bethelightindarkness
www.linkedin.com/in/be-the-light-foundation-84a116219
www.instagram.com/bethelight1181

ANGIE MONKO

Wounded to Worthy: Lessons from an Angel

My baby was ready now.

It was 2:00 a.m. on Thursday, April 18, 1996. I woke up to go to the bathroom. As I sat down on the toilet, water gushed. *Oh my god!* My water had broken. I wasn't due for another week, but my baby was ready *now*. I immediately told my husband, Rob, and we packed for the hospital. I was strangely calm.

I'd been imagining what Maddie would look like. What color eyes would she have? What would her personality be like? Would she be reserved and introverted like me, or more humorous and outgoing like her dad? All I knew was that I loved this little thing and was beyond excited to meet her.

I was admitted into my room. Rob had to leave to care for our dog, Maggie, but my mom was there, helping me with Lamaze breathing. That afternoon, I received oxytocin to speed up my labor.

Once the contractions started, I had to hold back the incredibly strong urge to push because my doctor still wasn't there. I was furious! He *finally* arrived around the same time Rob did!

In the delivery room, it only took three pushes to eject Maddie into the world at 3:18 p.m. She seemed to fly out of me.

They took her over to a table, cleaning her tiny six-pound, nine-ounce body. Smaller than I expected, as Rob was a big guy, and I'm not small. Strangely, I don't recall them bringing her to me to bond.

Rob, along with Maddie's grandparents, took turns holding her that evening. I was pretty exhausted and slept through the night. The next morning, doctors informed us, "We are going to have to send Maddie to St. Louis Children's Hospital because she has a distended stomach. This happens sometimes, and we need to know why." We were as shocked, disoriented, and disappointed as we'd been excited to take her home.

Hospitals don't do much on the weekends. We had to wait three grueling days before receiving the results of a sweat test, which would let us know if Maddie had cystic fibrosis (CF).

When we filed into the conference room on that cold, rainy Monday, April 22, we felt the dense energy and saw the long faces of five doctors in white coats. This couldn't be good. They confirmed our greatest fear. Maddie had CF, a chronic, progressive, fatal genetic disease that affects the lungs and digestion.

After being on a high from bringing a new life into the world, full of hopes and expectations of how we'd love Maddie, nurture her, connect with her, and watch her grow into a beautiful young woman, we were deflated, devastated.

When Rob and I got home that night, we held each other and sobbed. We were terrified about what this horrible disease would do to our sweet Maddie. Would she suffer? We would certainly suffer watching her in pain.

She continued to grow into a beautiful little baby, with plump cheeks, the most gorgeous blue eyes you've ever seen, and Shirley Temple, light-brown curls. From the outside, she was like any other little girl. We adjusted to the new normal, and life went on.

I was commuting over an hour each way to my job in St. Louis. My marriage had been strained before Maddie was born. I'd dated Rob, who was twelve years older, for seven years before we got married. I had been subconsciously seeking a father figure to compensate for being neglected and wounded by my dad. I always felt unsafe because of how he'd released his temper on my mom.

I was twenty-seven years old, feeling resentful and disconnected from my husband. I had over-given and taken over responsibility for our financial security up until Maddie was born. Even though we fought a lot because we both had strong opinions, I stayed quiet about my most vulnerable feelings. I didn't want to be intimate with him anymore. I was resentful of what I perceived as his lack of ambition, his childishness, and the cruel things he would say. Wasn't I the one holding things together? I was so tired.

I betrayed myself in many ways. I left a church I was involved in because I was told it was a "childish dependence" on God. I left behind friends because Rob didn't like them. He tried to control how much I saw my mom because he didn't like her.

I allowed myself to be taken advantage of and treated like a doormat. Life felt like all work and no play. Having a child with special needs added to my stress. It was overwhelming. I gave up.

I asked Rob for a divorce and joint custody, and he said, "Over my dead body."

I didn't have the strength or courage to fight him. My low self-worth drove me to my biggest self-betrayal. I gave him physical and legal custody of Maddie when she was almost two years old. I was more concerned about protecting his feelings than I was worried about the impact on Maddie because I felt guilty for wanting the divorce. I told myself she'd be fine, that he loved her.

I allowed him to hire an attorney who only represented him. He reassured me that he wanted me to have a relationship with Maddie, but thirty days after the ink dried on the divorce decree, he said, "You won't get one spoon out of the house."

I hit an all-time low. I felt incredibly guilty for giving him custody and stupid for trusting his word. I went on a quest to figure out how I could have been so reckless with my most precious relationship, my daughter. I had to heal my low self-worth, my deep woundedness that tricked me into believing I didn't deserve to fight for her.

This was the beginning of my shift from feeling wounded and broken to feeling worthy of being Maddie's mom. Feeling like I was worthy of being happy. I began doing the inner work—journaling, praying, asking God to help me heal myself.

For the next eleven years, I continued to see Maddie every other weekend, on holidays and summer visits. Our time together was absolutely precious to both of us. We clung to each other because our time was limited.

Maddie asked to move in with me when she was eleven, and Rob's response was "absolutely not," but we were determined to make it happen. I taught her Emotional Freedom Techniques, visualization, and meditation to empower her to manifest this desire. I was doing the same. Our intentions paid off, and on July

9, 2009, Maddie (now thirteen) moved in with me, my husband, Steve (I remarried in 2002), and his daughter, Chelsea (a year older than Maddie).

We were ecstatic. Over the years, from the time the girls were four and five, we made sweet memories together, traveling all over the world (Australia, Hawaii, Paris, Colorado, Maine, Key West), playing, laughing, bonding, sharing our deepest thoughts and feelings.

Maddie remained healthy for many years. She was fifteen the first time she went into the hospital. That's when she began taking IV antibiotics, which impacted her gut and immune system, requiring more frequent hospital stays. She developed more scar tissue on her lungs with each CF exacerbation.

Maddie was fiercely loyal to and loved her family and friends, her dogs, turtles, and frogs, and even owned a bearded dragon named Speedy. She loved contorting her beautiful countenance into the ugliest, silliest troll faces, and she told lame jokes that were so flat, they'd make you laugh even more.

She was five-foot, two-inches, little and wiry, weighing one hundred and thirty pounds at her heaviest and only eighty-eight at her thinnest. She loved to dance, pumping her clenched fists in and out over her chest, to the rhythm of hip hop and rap. Oh my, did she love to eat and cook! We had so much fun planning and preparing meals and savoring our delightful creations.

She became the youngest Certified Healing Code Practitioner, with a true talent to help others heal. Yet she was human, full of insecurity and low-self-worth at times, afraid of suffering, knowing in her heart she wasn't going to live long. She truly valued quality time with her family and friends.

August 2018, we began a Power of Eight® Healing Circle for her. Twelve of her closest people gathered every Saturday, setting intentions for her to heal and finally be free. This Healing Circle helped her transition into another realm, where she is truly free. Maddie died on Friday, October 26, 2018. She was twenty-two years old. She's with me every day. This story is dedicated to my Maddie Angel. She taught me to be a loving self-advocate, because, according to Maddie, "Life is too short to be anyone other than yourself."

Angie Monko founded Harmony Harbor Coaching in 2008. She is a Conscious Women's Divorce and Loss Coach, guiding women into healing after divorce and loss so they and their children can move forward stronger and happier into their next chapter. Angie's work creates a safe space for women as they become loving advocates and learn to honor and respect themselves. In her workshops, retreats, private coaching and online programs, Angie helps women become healthy and create vital role models for their children, family, and friends— their sphere of influence. By communicating their needs, managing their energy, and feeling supported, they break the chains of the past and step fully into their power. Angie has certifications in Emotional Freedom Techniques, Hypnosis, and the Healing Codes, and is well-versed in Donna Eden energy medicine, all designed to heal the heart and align energy.

www.harmonyharbor.com
angie@harmonyharbor.com
www.facebook.com/angela.monko
www.pinterest.com/harmonyharborcoaching
www.facebook.com/The-Collaborative-Divorce-Alliance-100317329121894
www.facebook.com/HarmonyHarborHypnosis

HEIDI CECIL

Why Are You Waiting?

I'm lying in bed, wondering if I'm breathing.
I need to stay awake to be sure.

It's September. Fall is my favorite season, and while I'm checking to make sure I'm breathing, I wonder if I will be around to experience the autumn colors, the crisp air.

How had I let myself turn into this disaster-pretending-to-be-me at forty-seven? I hadn't lived my life, yet here I was, desperate, unhappy, and unhealthy in my body, mind, and spirit. I remembered I had a doctor's appointment that morning, if I could just keep breathing!

I made it to my appointment, and my doctor was very compassionate. He did what he was trained to do. He prescribed antidepressants and antianxiety drugs.

"I'm having panic attacks," I told him. "I can't take those things. There has to be another way."

"You can go to the hospital. Can you drive yourself?"

Knowing I only had one chance, I said, "Yes," then ditched the hospital.

Next, I tried something new. I called my best friend of a billion years, and, snot-faced and sobbing, told her, "I need help." I tried to explain what I was going through, but I could hardly talk.

"I'm on my way," she calmly replied.

I sort of packed. Mostly I sprawled across my bed, sobbing. My heart was broken, my spirit was crushed. Oh, and the guilt—so many people needed me. I couldn't even take care of myself. I was a mess.

She hugged me when I opened the door. I sagged, both of us crumbling onto the floor. She let me cry, then held me until I caught my breath.

All I felt was love from her. Why? How could she love me? I used to be a good mom, wife, daughter, sister, friend. I had done good things in my life, but none of that mattered anymore. How could anyone love me? I didn't.

I knew my answers weren't at the hospital. I was terrified of being caught up in a cycle of medicines, side effects and possible addictions. I'd had them all at one point or another: medications, alcohol, food, bad relationships. I could not afford another unhealthy addiction—physically, mentally or financially. I knew I needed to change everything in my life but could not imagine where to begin.

She took me home with her. On the drive, I kept going over all the reasons I couldn't leave my life. (Notice that I used *leave*, not *end*.) I'm a single mom with kids and pets. My youngest is struggling. I have a full-time job. I'm barely hanging on to my house. My brother and I take turns caring for our dad, who is sick. There were no easy answers.

About twenty-four hours in, I announced, "I caused this. I caused all of this." She smiled.

"I can't breathe. I can't function." I'm stumbling through her house I've been in a million times, unable to find anything. She hands me things I need. We drink tea in the front yard. I feed her chickens and cry. She says funny things that make me laugh.

"I have to get back to my life, right?" Not yet.

Through some very creative planning and arranging with amazing friends and family members, my friend helped put my responsibilities in the hands of others.

She said I was to "trust that everything will work out in the end in the best way possible."

That was really terrifying. That would mean letting go of all those ideas about how women should behave. We just suck it up and go on. That's what I had done, until I wasn't able to breathe.

I had been in my own damn way! What? Getting out of my own damn way meant stepping away from my life for an undetermined amount of time.

I'm great at making bad decisions, and while this could have been one more bad decision, I knew I had to do it, and that if I didn't, I wouldn't make it. I had followed all the rules the best I could. I had the American dream. God in my life. Husband, kids, pets, house, cars, income. I had happy moments, but I wasn't really a joyful person. I was overweight, overstressed, overstimulated, overmedicated, and overprocessed. If that's the dream, I don't need it! *I was over it!*

Although the days and nights that followed were not easy, they were *exquisite*. I gave up everything, without question. I let go of every "normal" idea and tried new things. I submitted to a healthy body, mind, and spirit, and once I started letting go, all three kicked in!

Here's how it played out.

I wake up at dawn (I've never been a morning person) to a rooster crowing. I feel light, delightful.

"What is this feeling?" I ask as I look for my shoes. I throw the door open and run downstairs to get the chicken feed. I don't care that no one is up yet. I start tea and then head outside to feed the chickens. As they break into a run when they see me, I laugh with the most liberating feeling I have had in a long time.

"Joy? Did I just feel joy? Over chickens? Over anything?" I'm talking out loud—to myself or the chickens—and smiling. I spend days and nights healing, doing therapy, eating wholesome foods, playing with dogs, turning off the outside world and its noise. I prayed, sang, laughed, and danced. I did it anytime and anywhere I felt like it. Was this what it felt like to take care of yourself? That's exactly what it was. I was taking care of myself and finding little pieces of joy.

It was the hardest thing I've done in my life. It's not easy to admit defeat and start over. There were consequences. Good and bad.

But I felt the changes inside myself. They were multiplying by the minute. My eyes were starting to sparkle, and I was getting color in my cheeks. Weight started to come off, and the fog in my brain started to lift. I was feeling a little confident. I started removing limitations I was unaware I had even put in place.

Just as I'm ready to slingshot back into my life, October blasts us with a crazy ice storm, taking out the power for two weeks. Dad's nursing home loses power along with our homes, so my brother and I take turns caring for him in a hotel that had power. And I return to work.

I was so grateful I had that space to heal, breathe, and learn to love myself again before all that came next. In December, Dad passed away. Seeing that I was afraid of losing this fragile hold on my new life, my brother reminded me, "Dad is where he wants to be, and the best way to honor him is to live your life. Life is for the living, sissy. Seriously, don't stay stuck indoors! Get out and do something every time you have a chance."

I agreed. it was time to step up my game. I made plans to take my daughter on a trip, and my brother planned a camping trip with his son. My brother went on his trip the night before.

As my youngest daughter and I prepared to head out, my older daughter came flying through the house, crying, "Your brother is at the lake. Paramedics are working on him. It's not good, momma."

Then my mom called. My little brother didn't make it.

Time stood still. This was the deepest loss I've ever faced. I didn't know how I'd get through it. But I did. Mostly.

I managed my life by focusing on joy. I made decisions and acted on them. Big ones, little ones, hard ones. I said yes to unimaginable things, and I did them. I sold my house and said "so long" to the American dream and normal way of life.

That friend I came all undone with? We closed a deal on the most beautiful property in Southeastern Oklahoma that is not just our home but our shared business: a campground constructed for delight and enchantment.

That missing piece? It was in me all along. I had it. I surrendered. I got out of my own way in every way. Body. Mind. Spirit. Once my mind was clear, my body was able to drop the weight and stop the unhealthy collection of ailments that slowed me down. My spirit reengaged, my attitude changed, and my soul set on fire!

I had the choice to remain in pain and misery. We all do. I could have waited for the chaos to end and life to *settle down*. If I had, time would have slipped anyway. I would not be here, enjoying this exact joyful moment!

Why are you waiting? Life is for the living! Find your joy! It's there. Love yourself enough to let go of all the things that hold you back. Who cares what anyone else thinks? Let yourself be drenched in joy. You know it's true; you already have everything you need inside of you.

Heidi Cecil was born and raised in the Oklahoma City area, where she was certain she would raise her family and live forever. Little did she know, she would create a massive shift in her life that would take her on a more magical journey. Heidi started a new business at the end of 2021 with her business partner, operating a unique campground (opening this year) for others to rest, restore, experience the enchantment of life, and discover themselves. Heidi has three children, ages sixteen, twenty-four, and twenty-six. She spent eighteen years managing a retail chain, then moved into her insurance career. She loves taking care of her clients at the Wood Insurance Agency as she continues to help others find a zest-filled life!

www.facebook.com/camptbd
www.woodagencyokc.com/

DR. AMY HORN

Set Your Soul Ablaze

"She's a bit too much," said the universe never.

If you have read this far into this anthology and are not convinced that anything is possible, buckle up and keep reading. *You hold the power to be and do anything you want.* Today and all the days ahead of you are, simply, up to you.

Have you ever had an aha moment? A moment in time that either stands still or "it" all comes together and makes sense? An "in the zone" moment? Those moments fuel my fire. Set my soul ablaze. Connect me to a bigger and mightier power than I can explain. I wish I could say that it has always been the case. That I've always been like this, but there is no story if that's the case. Here's a little secret: I have always been like this, *I just wasn't always aware.* The same is likely true for you too. You have the same power as me. Let me tell you how I became aware of my power and how you can find yours.

Because talking is a hobby of mine and I cross paths with many people in my practice, I tell many people that I've lived my life in three stages.

Oblivious

The First Stage looked like this: I was who I was, but I wasn't aware. Think late teenager, early twenties, going about life, doing my thing, feeling "good" for the most part, and just oblivious to any other feeling than what was happening in the now.

My life dramatically changed by the time I turned twenty-five. Although graduating chiropractic school and becoming a wife and a mother were all exceptionally awesome things, I could feel a change in my demeanor. Over the course of a few years, babies two and three came along, and I was chugging away: mom, wife, doctor, sometimes doctor, mom, wife, sometimes *Mom, Mom, Mom*! By societal standards, my life was out of balance.

Stuck-ed-ness

This was the Second Stage of my life: I was acutely aware that I didn't feel like "me" anymore. So relatable. I've heard it now many times in my practice: "I just don't feel like myself anymore." This is the stage of stuck-ed-ness. Groundhog day. Showing up, doing your thing, only to go home, go to bed, and then do it all over again tomorrow. The "hamster wheel of life," or so we're sold. I could feel my life energy being sucked out of me. It frustrated the hell out of me.

"But," I told myself, "I'm supposed to be a great doctor, a great mom, and a great wife." I wasn't terrible at any of it, I just felt like a robot. I was so not in tune with who I was or my life's purpose. I was a version of myself as a human doing and not a human being. Yep, that phrase hit me like a punch in the face.

I was invited at some point in the course of these few years to hear a life coach give a presentation. I tend to be an all-in kind of person with the newest fads, while at the same time living a life that generally goes against the grain. Meaning, I'm willing to give it a try if everyone is talking about it or no one knows much about it. So here I am sitting in a classroom setting with a few other people, and Mr. Life Coach starts off with an exercise. "Shout out a description of who you are."

The answers were flying, many similar to mine: wife, mom, doctor, friend, husband, lawyer, teacher . . . you get the picture. The board was full.

And then our presenter said, "Ah! Yes! Somehow I knew you'd say that! Now, tell me *who* you are, because this board is full of everything you do."

Oh. OK. Then that squirmy feeling started creeping in. Do you know the one—that feeling of being uncomfortable? Yes, both physically and emotionally uncomfortable. Exposed. Unsure. "Am I the only one that doesn't know the answer?" I waited in silence as did everyone else. And slowly answers came pouring in, albeit general answers: kind, funny, calm, busy. Intriguing.

Awareness

I hadn't really thought about it until that moment. Who am I? I took a chance on an adventure outside of my comfort zone and signed up for the program the life coach offered. That was the beginning of what I call Stage Three of my life. I remember the exact moment it happened. The simple questions I answered.

"Describe your best day. Your very best day, what does it look like? What does it feel like? Now, describe you on that day. What qualities do you have? Facial expressions? How do you act?"

In that moment, I defined who I was, my being. Two new questions framed every decision moving forward: "Will this support who I am? Will this support who I want to be?" If the answer was no, I simply didn't participate.

Stage Three: I became *aware* of who I am. At my core. What makes me tick. The answer was always there; my mission was to uncover it. My hope is that my words inspire you to channel your fire. Your purpose. Your being. It's in there. I promise.

Once you discover your being-ness, it's hard not to share the magic. Who wouldn't want to feel this feeling? Who wouldn't want to do the work? I would constantly hear things like "You're so lucky" or "It must be nice," as if my circumstances were a result of luck. Not so much. I remember complaining to a mentor at a chiropractic seminar. "There just isn't enough time in the day. I am trying to work and exercise and get the kids ready for school." His response to me was another honest-to-God, *life*-changing moment.

"We all have the same twenty-four hours in our day," he said. "You get to choose how you spend them."

The lightbulb in my head went off. Yes. My circumstances were different because of my choices. That was the push I needed. I chose, in that moment, to get up an hour earlier the next morning. Exercise would be first in my day while everyone was sleeping. I would set that time aside in the wee hours of the morning instead of crossing it off my to-do-but-undone list at the end of the day.

Game changer for me. Read: I made the choice and took an action to do something different to get the result I wanted. Do Not Read: "I must get up at four a.m."

Was it easy? No. Was I uncomfortable? Yes. Tired at first? Hell yes. Slept in my exercise clothes sometimes? You know it! The less thinking at four a.m., the better! Morning exercise sets the tone of my day. In my professional, heavily researched, cognitive awareness, exercise releases neurotransmitters that balance mood and overall wellbeing. Yes? Yes! I was setting myself up to be in the flow, even on the days that threw curveballs.

In my practice as a chiropractor, I see people that are uncomfortable with where they currently are in life. Whether it is physical or emotional pain, people seek my help to feel better. It starts out that way at least. It's a whole conversation in my office.

"What is this preventing you from doing?" I ask. "If you felt one hundred percent, what would you want to do?" Off we go.

Every day I say, "We take better care of our cars than we do our bodies." And every day people nod in agreement. We have the oil changed and tires rotated because we know if we do not, our cars would be less efficient and break down faster. Preventative care? Sounds like it.

However, preventative health care in our mainstream model currently looks like making sure we're just not sick. Blood pressure "normal," lungs sound clear, no lumps or bumps. Checkmark healthy. But wait. We don't feel healthy. I mean, we may not feel sick, but we lack energy and vibrance. Don't we need to ask how to keep blood pressure normal and avoid lumps or bumps? Who is teaching us that? That sounds like prevention. Which brings me to the power of our human body!

All day every day, I get to describe the power of the brain and nervous system. It doesn't get anywhere near the credit it deserves. The electrical system of the body, the very core of our being-ness, is overlooked until it's overstressed and broken. No wonder we feel "disconnected," "not like ourselves," or "just not good." My circumstances were different because my choices were.

Harness. Your. Power.

Get right with your power. For me that looks like chiropractic adjustments, meditation, journaling, and exercise. My friends add yoga, acupuncture, and massage. Some add energy work and life coaching.

Train. Your. Brain.

That is the secret. Train your brain to overcome, power on, be still and connected, find the solution for right now. That is your choice every day. Every day you practice and put it into action, you get better at it until it becomes second nature. You become aware of your being and who you are. Then, what seems like magic or luck simply happens.

I put this practice to work many years back. My oldest son was eleven years old and played volleyball for his school team. My best friend and I coached this team together beginning when the kids were nine and continuing until they were fourteen. Luckily (but really not), we were at the same place in our careers and shared common insights. She, running her own business, had learned the same mindset "tactics" that I had. Together, we brought what we learned and practiced to our group of eleven-year-old boys.

The Shift: Setting the Soul Ablaze

The shift happened when my desire to want or be something different than the current standard was greater than the pain to achieve it. We all hold the same power. Peel back the layers, get real with who you really are, and lock in to your greatness. The world is calling you to be fully alive in your human being-ness. To set your soul ablaze.

The Takeaway: A Winning Mindset

You can put it to practice in your own life. What worked for a team of fifth-grade boys works for everyone. Our team had talent. They had a willingness to show up and work hard. They had a willingness to change what wasn't working and repeat what was. What we taught them was a winning mindset. We won the highest honors that year. The first of four available honors. It was exciting and exhilarating. It felt dang good to win. We began our sixth-grade year the same as our previous year: What is our end goal? And collectively our *big* end goal was to win highest honors all four years.

Instead of picking up a volleyball and practicing the mechanics of the game, we practiced the mechanics of the mind. The intuitive power of being. We closed our eyes and heard the sounds of a crowd celebrating, we visualized a scoreboard with our winning score. We saw in our minds the banner that hung on the wall, a testament to our accomplishment. We pictured it as if it had already happened, experienced the feelings we would feel when it did happen, and held the belief of it happening at the forefront of our minds. We won that year too. And all four years, just like we set out to do. It really is that easy.

Dr. Amy Horn is a chiropractic physician in the suburbs of St Louis, Missouri. Among her greatest accomplishments are her husband, Ken, and children Kade, Kannon, and Annie. As a devoted healer and lover of life, Amy spends her time perfecting the art of chiropractic, being in service to her patients, and adventuring with her family and friends. Self-described as an energetic dreamer, she brings a distinct passion to everything she does, her list ranging from gardener, boot camp leader and volleyball coach to writer, employer, doctor, and mom. Simply put, she is grateful for life and everything that comes with it . . . and not afraid to share it. It is in connection Amy finds herself fully alive. It is a humbling experience to put one's life story into words, but Amy asks, "Why else are we here, if not to make the world a better place?"

www.abundanthealthstl.com/
www.facebook.com/abundanthealthstl
www.instagram.com/abundanthealthstl/

DARLYSHIA MENZIE

RELEASE THEM:
The Power of Forgiveness

"What doesn't kill you makes you stronger." I beg to differ.

Strength has nothing to do with near-death experiences and everything to do with willingness, agility, and the ability to shift at any given moment. Strength results from being resilient in difficult situations. Strength is the byproduct of intentionality. Strength is choosing to press forward when everything in you wants to quit. I've learned, "When I persevere, I am stronger."

It all started for me in the summer of 2020, the year of the pandemic. The world was in a health crisis, and I was having a few personal challenges of my own. Having experienced some relationship woes, I was stuck trying to shake the emotional consequences of unresolved issues.

To know me is to know that I value relationships and hate to have anything misunderstood, unresolved, or misinterpreted, especially with people I care about. Nevertheless, that seemed to keep coming up. One person after another kept talking about how I functioned in our relationships, so I decided it was time to figure out why this was happening repeatedly and address it.

This is where my choices kicked in. I could choose to ignore what they were saying and count it as hearsay, gossip, or just them misunderstanding me. Conversely, I could choose to do the mature thing and address it head-on. I chose the latter. I made the tough decision to get transparent with myself and actually

234

listen to and assess the feedback that was coming to me about the role I played in relational distancing.

I actually had to view these comments outside of my own lens. I'll admit—I was feeling like a victim. My feelings were hurt, and I was confused. I couldn't understand how people who said they loved me and had known me for so long could so misinterpret my character and hold it against me.

I didn't want to feel like a victim anymore, so I prayed and asked God to show me the truth in what was being said and to expose the "why" behind emotional triggers—mine and theirs. God answered my prayers and began to show me all that I had requested.

I was surprised, to say the least, and a great deal ashamed at how I had dismissed others' feelings and been neglectful over time. I was disappointed in how I had mishandled the relationships with people whom I'd said I loved and valued. I was sorrowful and wanted to make things right.

Here is my second choice—the choice to ask for forgiveness or the choice to keep what I had discovered to myself and pretend nothing ever happened. I chose the former.

I'd do it all over again. This is where my strength kicked in. Choice after choice. I was compelled to make an intentional shift in perspective and take intentional action. I could have made excuses, but then I wouldn't have been OK. It wouldn't have been enough to go on with business as usual. I put my big-girl pants on and started making phone calls.

Tough conversation after tough conversation went like this:

"I realized why you said I made you feel _____. I failed to _____ and can now understand how that caused you to lose confidence in me."

"What I did was _____. What you really wanted was _____. I was dealing with _____ and it clouded my ability to be a better friend to you, and for that I apologize. You are [add something positive about that person as friend/colleague/partner]. I value _____ about you and [add an affirmation that authentically speaks to their character]."

It was a lot to internalize, but I wanted to repair the relationships and mature in the process. As I admitted to my role in each relationship, it got easier to face them and myself. My load got lighter; theirs did too. My heart filled with peace; theirs did too. I was no longer burdened with the feeling of having let people down who I cared about. They were finally feeling fully seen by me and appreciated my awareness. I began to see a brighter future for myself, one without feeling guilty or wondering if I would be the source of things getting messed up.

For a long time, I questioned if I could be a good friend. Being able to receive feedback without bitterness—and actually be real with myself concerning that feedback—liberated me from that doubt. I won my friends back! I earned their trust! Taking the time to listen to them, acknowledge their feelings, own my part, ask for forgiveness, and make a change restored the relationship. Restoration was a direct result of shifting with intention! That intentional shift was forgiveness.

I want to talk to you about the power of forgiveness. I've heard that being unable to forgive is like drinking poison and expecting the other person to die. I've also heard that forgiveness is not only for the other person but also for you. Life can change for you in the best ways possible when you learn to let go of the things that have hurt you, the people who have disappointed you, and the things that didn't go the way you expected. It's also important and necessary to learn how to forgive yourself and walk in wholeness. To forgive others is to heal yourself. To forgive yourself is to welcome more life, new life, greater life.

My forgiveness journey in 2020 changed my whole life. I no longer have a victim mentality. I no longer blame people for how they feel about me. I'm no longer bitter in my heart about people's expressed disappointment in me. I no longer have lingering questions that last for weeks, months, years—questions that I am not able to address. Forgiveness allowed me to heal and open myself up to what is to come. No guilt. No shame. No regret. I can see clearer now and focus on my future.

As a result of this shift, God has entrusted me with new and different things! New relationships! New opportunities! New creative ideas! New freedom in my heart! Honestly, this experience opened me up to a new life. No drama! Really a new life. And I have more time because I'm not second-guessing how I show up in relationships or wondering and worrying about what could have been. I'm wholly focused on the here and now, along with what's ahead, and there's no time to slow down.

I have more gratitude. I'm able to improve the relationships that I'm currently in. I notice when I fall into old habits much faster, and I can correct myself much quicker. My conversations with my friends are more open and honest. I no longer feel like I need to compare, hide, or censor myself. I don't have to fight to be liked.

Forgiveness has allowed me to soar beyond my wildest expectations. No one wants to feel the isolation and confusion that comes with muddled relationships, but we all do it. We all have someone in our lives who we do not see eye-to-eye with, for whatever reason, and it's hard to be with them. Holding on to grudging resentment only makes matters worse and impacts everyone's quality of life.

Release them! Release them from the punishment of judgment. Release them from the mistakes they have made over time. Release them from their consistent mistakes and disappointments. You are the only one who can release them from the prison of your heart. While you're at it, forgive yourself for holding on to the hurt for so long. Forgive yourself for becoming someone else while angry, for letting them control your actions. Forgive yourself for the time wasted on something that wasn't adding to your happiness, joy, and freedom.

If I could give you any wisdom, it would be to *keep working on you until you become someone you love.* When you come to love yourself and the life you live, imperfections and all, anything is possible. You truly can soar! Loving you and loving your life does not happen by accident; it happens on purpose—it happens intentionally. Choose to have the uncomfortable conversations. Pray. Self-reflect. Give your best effort. Laugh. Give and receive forgiveness. Extend and accept grace. Embody strength.

It takes strength to face ourselves in the mirror every single day and choose the best of us to be in a world filled with everyone else's life and business. I choose to ask the hard questions, and you can too. It will all be worth it, because you are.

Darlyshia Menzie is the owner and CEO of *Fervent Servant LLC*, a coaching and consulting practice whose mission is to get people excited about their lives by investigating and investing in their personal and spiritual growth. As a dynamic, transformational speaker, published author, Certified Life Coach, curriculum consultant, and real estate agent, Darlyshia brings energy, high expectation, and zeal to every encounter. She believes that growth only happens with intention and an honest assessment of self. With that in mind, she empowers others to take responsibility for their lives and do what's necessary to live with purpose every single day. Darlyshia started her business with a desire and personal commitment to become the resource she needed in different stages of her life, making her a true Fervent Servant. Her motto is: "Live with Intention. Serve with Passion."

www.darlyshiamenzie.com/connect